Philosophy for Life

Also available from Continuum:

Great Thinkers A–Z, edited by Julian Baggini and Jeremy Stangroom

What We Can Never Know, by David Gamez

What Philosophers Think, edited by Julian Baggini and Jeremy Stangroom

What More Philosophers Think, edited by Julian Baggini and Jeremy Stangroom

Philosophy for Life

Rupert Read

Edited by M. A. Lavery

continuum

Continuum International Publishing Group
The Tower Building
11 York Road
London SE1 7NX
www.continuumbooks.com

80 Maiden Lane
Suite 704
New York
NY 10038

British Library Cataloguing-in-Publication Data
A catalogue record for this book is available from the British Library.

ISBN: PB: 0-8264-9560-5
9780826495600
HB: 0-8264-9609-1
9780826496096

Library of Congress Cataloging-in-Publication Data
Read, Rupert J., 1966–
Philosophy for life/by Rupert Read; edited by M. A. Lavery. p. cm.

ISBN-13: 978-0-8264-9609-6
ISBN-10: 0-8264-9609-1
ISBN-13: 978-0-8264-9560-0
ISBN-10: 0-8264-9560-5
1. Ethics.   2. Conduct of life.   I. Lavery, M. A.   II. Title.

BJ301.R43 2007
128-dc22

2007001405

Typeset by BookEns Ltd, Royston, Herts.
Printed and bound in Great Britain by The Cromwell Press, Trowbridge, Wiltshire

Contents

Acknowledgements

This book owes its existence to many fine people, none the least of whom are the publishers and editors who permitted previously published material to be reprinted below.

Chapter 1 is reprinted from parts of 'Nature, culture, *ecosystem*: or, the priority of environmental ethics to epistemology and metaphysics', originally included in *Feminist Interpretations of Ludwig Wittgenstein*, edited by Naomi Scheman and Peg O'Connor, and published by the Penn State Press in 2002.

Chapter 2 contains material reprinted with permission by the *Eastern Daily Press*.

Chapter 3 contains excerpts from 'The centrality of the concept of "practice" among Quakers', originally included in *Quaker Religious Thought*, issue 86, in 1996.

Chapter 5 contains excerpts from 'Is forgiveness ever possible at all?', originally published in *Literature and Philosophy: A Guide to Contemporary Debates*, edited by David Rudrum and published by Palgrave Macmillan in 2006; and 'Is forgiveness possible? The cases of Thoreau and Rushdie (on) (writing) the unforgivable', published in *Reason Papers*, issue 21.

Chapter 6 is reprinted from parts of 'How I learned to love and hate Noam Chomsky', in *Philosophical Writings*, issues 15 and 16, published in 2000 and 2001 respectively. It also contains material used, with permission, from the *Eastern Daily Press*.

Chapter 7 contains material from 'Barsham and Bronson (eds),

The Lord of the Rings and philosophy', a book review published in *Philosophical Psychology* in 2005.

Chapter 8 contains portions of 'Martin Warner, A philosophical study of T. S. Eliot's *Four Quartets*', published in *Philosophical Books* in 2004.

All contents were written by Rupert Read.

Editor's Introduction

'Where philosophers fear to tread?'; or, From applied philosophy to philosophy applied

This book aims to go where philosophy is typically scared to venture: *into* the 'murky' domains of love, forgiveness, religious practice, our connections with animals, political dissidence, (particularly green) politics, revolutionary art – in short, areas of social and political thought often pushed aside in current academic discourse, perhaps thought to be too controversial or too 'soft'. The book aims both to deepen and enliven these topics with some sustained intellectual reflection and, mostly, to draw out the way their being marginalized misrepresents the complexity of their role in everyday life, the way they figure into our actual lived world. In other words, the goal here is to bring philosophy into real life in a way that a wide variety of readers may appreciate.

Perhaps another – possibly even better and more concise – way of looking at this collection of seemingly disparate essays is as an assault on the received understanding of applied philosophy, which could currently be roughly defined as 'philosophical work in a broadly analytic tradition which is intended to make a constructive contribution to problems' in 'areas of practical concern including environmental and medical ethics, the social implication of scientific and technological change, philosophical and ethical issues in education, law and economics'.[1] Here, Rupert Read works to supplant this view with an increasingly influential idea of philosophy *itself* as necessarily applied: philosophy not as a body of doctrine but as a practice, a vantage point from which life – as the totality of human existence, in all its mundanity and intricacy – is to be considered, and, more importantly, acted upon. (Marx famously said that philosophers have only *interpreted* the world, and that the point is to *change* it; Read thinks that philosophy can make it *natural* for one to want to change the world.) This project therefore argues that a proper conception of applied philosophy makes it inseparable from ethics and politics, and emphasizes the necessary role of politics, in the broadest sense of that word, in 'applying' philosophy.

This 'new' conception of philosophy has its origins in the work of Ludwig Wittgenstein, who is quite possibly the most important, and certainly the most undersold, ethicist in philosophy's last several hundred years at least. Wittgenstein's ethical explorations may be quite difficult for interested but uninitiated readers to understand, and with good reason. As Wittgenstein himself says, perhaps nothing at all can accurately be said about (his work in) ethics:

> My whole tendency and I believe the tendency of all men who ever tried to write or talk Ethics or Religion was to run against the boundaries of language. This running against the walls of our cage is perfectly, absolutely hopeless. Ethics, so far as it springs from the desire to say something about the ultimate meaning of life, the absolute good, the absolute valuable, can be no science. What it says does not add to our knowledge in any sense.[2]

He goes on: 'But it is a document of a tendency in the human mind which I personally cannot help respecting deeply and I would not for my life ridicule it'. This last states clearly the lifelong commitment Wittgenstein had to such explorations despite the relative dearth of overt discussions of ethics within his texts, and the (above) clearly stated major tenet of his linguistic philosophy: that ethics is not something that can truly be discussed in language.

Instead, a Wittgensteinian disposition towards ethics conceives of it as life. Let me be clear about this: it is not a part of life, not something we choose to be involved in occasionally or when we are doing only certain things, not like play-acting – a costume we put on and take off – where there are clear indications of when and how we should do so. Instead, ethics is the manner of our living. In some ways it could be explained as being a description of our lives. At our best, it is the way we describe our lives to ourselves. This is why both 'What it says does not add to our knowledge in any sense' – his words – and it 'is something that cannot be discussed in language' – my paraphrase of his implication.

There is perhaps a more formal/technical/'philosophical' way of putting it: for Wittgenstein, knowledge is not just a matter of fact. Knowledge is *normative*. (See, for instance, Chapter 1, below.) And meaning is not just a matter of fact; meaning is *ethical*. (See, for instance, Chapter 7 on Chomsky below.)

But what does it mean, exactly, to say things like this? What does Wittgenstein's philosophy amount to?

Because of its radically different nature from received forms of philosophy, Wittgenstein's method is extremely difficult to compress for synoptic presentation. Great care must be taken here. Many Wittgensteinians, even Dr Read himself, may not agree with what I have said so far. Perhaps the only paraphrasing I can safely offer here is that a Wittgensteinian disposition leads us towards conceiving of ethics as something we do – not as something we have or a body of doctrine to which we subscribe. An ethical examination forces us to look at our practices, at ourselves.

Thus, an immediate goal of this book (i.e. a prerequisite for the conceptual change about 'applied philosophy' detailed in brief above) is to provide several tangible examples of 'ethical' practice. Dr Read goes beyond 'applying' preconceived philosophical theories (like 'pragmatism', 'phenomenology', or 'utilitarianism') to highly specialized areas (like biomedicine, or business ethics) in favour of isolating philosophical examinations of everyday concerns – how we take our holiday, the news we 'consume', how we seek out the beautiful (and what we try to do with it!), love, and so on. In so doing he makes manifest how abandoning the idea of philosophy as a body of theory gives rise to a *more* valuable clarification of (our) thinking about the world and our place in it. To accomplish this, the author combines material – some previously published and much new – from both academic and 'popular' sources, such as his regular newspaper column and the newsletters of groups with which he is affiliated. As such, this book challenges the often unspoken 'ivory-tower' divide between scholastic critical thinking on the one hand and everyday principled action on the other.

This format can pose difficulties for a typical readerly aim: to find an easy cohesiveness in the sundry and possibly seemingly disparate chapters of this book. To some extent this challenge is necessary: one cannot adopt a new way of thinking until a wrong one is wrested away, and this process is almost always uncomfortable. But this discomfort is the key to properly understanding how the Wittgensteinian approach to ethics (and philosophy in general) is a natural successor to the current consensus by which these are understood; to understand, in short, how philosophy in the twenty-first century can be a philosophy for living. For everyday life.

Recall (my paraphrasing of) Wittgenstein's suggestion that ethics is a way of living. (There is a mandate for both philosophy and philosophers included in this running together of philosophy and living – one that applies both to this book and to its author). So long as we want to live in society, we cannot avoid the question, the challenge, of an ethical life. We must simply live one or choose not to and accept the consequences. There are no third options[3] – except, of course, to go mad.

Read's book, by contrast, throughout offers us the prospect of a higher sanity. The urbane wisdom and the therapeutic [4] impact of philosophy might yet help to make life in the twenty-first century survivable, sane … even a pleasure! Truly worth living.

And if this book prompts just one person to adopt a saner life, and a happier one, it will have been worth producing.

I Environment

Editor's Introduction

We like to think of natural and environmental disasters as two different things: an environmental disaster is our, humans', fault; while a natural disaster, like Hurricane Katrina, well, that just 'happens'. Now, however, we have come to see something worse, something that is both natural *and* environmental disaster.

This is us: humans. This is our arrogantly, foolishly living out of line with nature; only there's a dangerous rub. Humans can never be out of nature's way. We are natural, even when we do seemingly 'unnatural' things. And there are prices. And we (and the rest of nature) pay them.

There are several links uniting the claim of the paragraphs above, which the first two chapters of this book draw out. The first is the mistaken and problematic position humans try to assign themselves with respect to nature – either to be outside it, or to constitute it fully. The humbling reality is that we are neither, and the first chapter, derived from an essay in *Feminist Interpretations of Ludwig Wittgenstein* (Penn State Press, 2002) explores this first point on what is hoped to be a journey towards ecological health: humans are part of a complex natural system in which all things affect each other, and must act accordingly.

The second chapter debunks in frightening detail the imagined gap between natural and environmental disasters: what else could the latter be other than the former? Informed by the notion that human action is as much a part of the natural sphere as animal action – the swinging from tree to tree of a baboon, for instance – this essay argues that it is ultimately our attempt to live outside this constraint, to grow our way out of it, that is a chimera with ironic consequences: the harder we try to escape our naturality – for instance, by air-conditioning our houses in the summer to escape the heat – the harder and faster that naturalness is reinforced for us. And if we try to build a bigger air conditioner to escape the global warming our last air conditioner contributed to, its capacity to cool us is soon outstripped by the additional heat it creates. And so (should?) we build another …

Here the first move away from thinking of philosophy as a collection of clever aphorisms, rules, theories or facts is initiated. Memorizing what this section says will do no good. Instead, this section must be experienced, in the way one silently watches the toys a child plays with when she doesn't know she is being watched. These are her values, the things we will want to share with her when we, ourselves, play. This section asks you to watch and play …

1 We Are Part of Our Ecosystem

'Man is born natural and is everywhere in culture ...'

My 'epigraph' might very naturally lead us to consider the following question: if it is true that humans are or were at the outset natural, and that it is our cultures and civilizations which have led to the Earth's increasing devastation, then how should we react to this devastation, if not by affirming Nature and severely questioning Culture? I want to suggest that there is something wrong about the phrasing of such questions as this. They continue a venerable but troubling intellectual tradition, which we may term for convenience the 'Nature vs Culture' debate (a debate which sits right alongside its close cousin, the nature–nurture debate). This debate involves further questions such as: which is responsible for the other? Does Nature provide the substance, and Culture just a few trimmings? Or is Nature fully constructed by Culture, materially (and 'metaphysically') a human artefact?

I wish to subvert the conversation which would have us continue to act as if the question 'Does Nature make Culture, or vice versa?' were a live one. I contend that the question is actually moribund, though not because it can be decisively answered one way or another. Rather, we need to re-orient the conversation.

It will be my contention that some of the major innovations in western philosophical thought in the twentieth century have long since provided the materials with which thoroughly to evade[1] the debate, not perpetuating obfuscation through the use of terms such as 'Nature' and 'Culture'. Are there more positive reasons why we should wish to end the Nature versus Culture debate? I believe so, and that they have to do with being able to say and do things which are environmentally ethical yet politically pragmatic (which is not to be equated with 'compromised'). Concretely, the possibility for which I will argue is that it is possible to re-forge our environment (including ourselves) in the best ways possible without trying forlornly to separate out which elements in that environment are 'genuinely natural'.

Somebody, a literary theorist eager to resolve interdisciplinary misunderstandings perhaps, might at this point wish to intervene: 'I can help end the debate: why not simply stress Culture, given the ubiquity of human construction of the world we live in? After all, the "hardest" of hard scientists is still at work in a community of inquiry, in a cultural setting; all of us are in the final analysis really creators and analysers of texts.' All the world's a text, and men and women merely its authors, as it were.

A reply must centre on the point that the conceptualization of Culture as all-pervasive, as if everything that humans touch turns to Culture, is highly problematic. The problem is: such a totalizing of Culture, if intended to play an explanatory or foundational role with regard to 'Nature', is ultimately empty.

In order to see this, one has to face a systematic ambiguity in the term 'construct', which alone gives the hypothetical proposal by the literary critic imagined above any plausibility. Namely, is it being envisaged that Civilization now limitlessly (re-) constructs Nature physically/materially, through our rapacious bio-technological power; or is a more fundamental sense of 'metaphysical' construction – through representational *categories*, or categories of thought – being envisaged? In the former sense, it is fairly obvious that some elements at least of Nature will remain impervious or antecedent to human construction. That is, humans cannot literally create or construct all (or even most) phenomena that we are inclined to call 'natural', even if it is possible to alter or destroy – to *re*construct, perhaps – many of them.

As for the latter, purely metaphysical sense of 'construct': if everything is culturally constructed, if *everything* can be placed within the 'cultural' category, then *nothing is explained* merely by invoking the 'social/cultural construction'. To say that Nature is totally culturally constructed in this sense is as yet actually to say *nothing*. This is so even if we think of the construction in question as done by means of the kind of idealized 'formalization' which overtook nature with Bacon and the 'Scientific Revolution'; that is, if the cultural construction in question is performed through scientific culture. For such construction can only be *re*construction, of some things; if it is supposed to extend to *everything*, then we are only expressing our determination not to allow anything to be described in terms other than scientific terms. We are not yet *saying anything* in those (or any other) terms.

In sum: any plausibility present in a strong Culturalist/Constructionist thesis evaporates once its inherent ambiguity is unmasked, when we realize that such a thesis is either false (if taken in the material sense) or vacuous (if taken in the metaphysical sense).

Let us now consider a related ambiguity in 'Nature'. As has already been hinted, some life-scientists and environmentalists tend to run together at least two senses of 'Nature' – one, in which Nature is everything, is inescapable and all-encompassing, because (emptily) totalized; a second, in which Nature is something certainly not wholly dominated by 'man', and is (at least potentially) separable from Culture. Only in the second sense can Nature have a normative role – as something to destroy, to fight, to master, to explore, to protect, to cherish, to become one with. In the first sense, everything we do, no matter what it is, is natural, to be described and explained 'naturalistically'. So one can draw no conclusions about whether to protect or respect something because it is part of nature in this first sense. Someone who totalizes nature has nothing to say to an opponent who claims, for instance, that aggression is a natural drive, or that causing mass devastation is just man's (or AIDS's) *natural* mission and other similar things.

It is the second sense of 'Nature' – according to which it is something that can be separated from 'Culture' – that is of particular interest in the present essay, because it has more ethical attractions: it might with some justice be thought to allow for the 'defence of Nature' position mentioned at the start of this chapter.[2] But again, this cuts both ways: Nature as the not-human can just as easily be attacked as defended. This second sense of 'Nature', then, is arguably one in which Nature has assumed the figure of 'Woman'. To take an instance of this, consider 'Gaia' imagery, currently very popular, with the new height of influence that its creator, James Lovelock, has reached. Doesn't such imagery always run the real risk of buying into the very stereotypes that one is trying elsewhere in one's work and life to overcome?[3] The worry is this: that Nature will be alternately respected, romanticized, raped and reclaimed repeatedly at least until this conceptualization of 'Her' is emended or ended. I am claiming that a risk intrinsic to the rhetoric of many ecologists, to (for example) the rhetoric of 'Mother Earth', is an immediate consequence of this being in the main *only the flip side of* the old rhetoric and strategies of 'mastering', 'conquering' and 'husbanding' (the last in particular a term extremely ripe for feminist analysis and deconstruction in this context). Those who support and cherish Nature (in the second sense given above) risk supporting only the long-running dialectic of adoration versus debasement, a 'dialectic' unlikely to rescue us from the ongoing devastation of the Earth. If one sees plainly the disambiguated senses of 'nature' which actually undergird this aspect of the debate, one will opt for neither; which, once again, is why those who invoke the figure of 'Nature' as female – whether to disrespect 'her', or to discover 'her', or to defy 'her', or to deify 'Her', or to delight in 'her' – often take care, again, not to effect such disambiguation. In short: Lovelock's 'Gaia' idea is deeply politically dangerous. To save the whales, to save the biosphere, to save the humans, it is not necessary to buy into plain silly gender-stereotypings of this rock in space on which we are all spinning.

Now, of course, some feminists employ the rhetoric of 'Mother Earth', and I would not wish to pretend that it can *never* be useful or empowering to do so. Whether or not one does so, one ought at least to show an *awareness* of the dangers of relying on either sense of 'Nature' as given above (or, worse still, on systematic ambiguity between them). Radical feminist Mary Daly is a major example of a feminist philosopher who has shown just such an acute awareness. The twin risks of making whatever happens natural (and therefore 'OK') on the one hand, and of viewing/figuring the Earth as female on the other, come together in Daly's unexpectedly savage critique of Lovelock's 'Gaia hypothesis'. The Gaia hypothesis apparently glorifies the beauty and wonder of the 'organism' that is the Earth-Goddess, while potentially allowing that (say) nuclear holocaust could be part of the natural process of our planet's 'development', i.e. it is compatible with the Gaia hypothesis that the Earth might 'protect herself' by fomenting mass destruction, mass extinction. One could read Mary Daly's gyn-ecological quest as that of the finding of a path towards making sense of our being 'always already' not just interdependent with but part of the planet, and even of each other. A sense of this profound non-alienation is what this chapter is all about. By contrast, the 'respect and love' adduced for Gaia by the proponents of the Gaia hypothesis reeks of a deep othering. It is as though people who are studying or glorifying the biosphere *cannot succeed in coherently and deeply envisioning themselves as part of it.*

According to my analysis thus far, then, 'pro-environmental' thinkers and activists, those who truly ('deeply') understand themselves to be of the world, have reason to be strongly suspicious of terms like 'Cultural Construction' and 'Nature'.

And one might worry that, even were our discourse or at least our understandings of these terms to be re-cast to take account of such suspicion, there might still be certain undesirable aspects of the 'Nature vs Culture' debate that we would be unable to avoid perpetuating. Particularly the alienation between – the irreconcilable separating off of – the two central terms of the debate or of any likely replacements for them. And thus the discursive situation would remain substantively the same, even though we might appear to have moved on to a less intrinsically problematic position. Though I cannot of course hope to illustrate this in every actual or possible case, let me tackle once more an apparent 'counter-example' to my suggestion that invoking 'Nature', for example, in a novel way is not enough to free one from the vicissitudes of the 'Nature vs Culture' dualism. The apparent counter-example comes from certain major strands in the green movement, in contemporary ecological consciousness and practice: it is said that 'man', the destructive animal, will technologize and colonize Nature into oblivion, unless a lesson of peace with the planet, of reunion with the oceanic Maternal figure (of Earth) is achieved. The point is that the Green movement runs the *risk*, the danger, of presupposing exactly the alienation of culture, of humans, from their/our natural surroundings that it *exists* to oppose and overcome (except – for contemporary westerners – possibly in some fantasized long-past era). The rhetoric of achieving peace with the planet, or of putting the Earth first ... all of this, its tactical value notwithstanding, is a problematic rhetoric still of *subject and object*, of actor and acted upon, of alienation.

My present suggestion is that we set aside envisioning this general terrain as one of Nature and Culture(s), that we endeavour *to overcome the Nature vs Culture debate altogether*. And this means, among other things, foreswearing so far as is possible any affirmative invocation of Nature and the natural per se.

'Inhabitants of the world unite: you have nothing to lose but (human) culture'

A key question for the remainder of the essay is in effect whether this 'epigraph' has any more use than – or makes any more sense than – that with which I commenced the essay. But if one's suspicions that it does not are well founded, still, *how* are we to evade the Nature-vs-Culture debate and the confusing academic and more-than-merely-academic disputes that it has bred?

The core of the proposal lying in some of the greatest philosophizing of the first half of the twentieth century (and explored in more concrete terms in some feminist and other political thought and activism) is simple; almost, but not quite, too simple. We have to overcome the trick of language that seduces us into seeing human cultures as in any sense necessarily opposed to 'what surrounds us'. But this is best effected *not* by totalizing Nature, as we saw earlier, or yet by totalizing Culture. We have instead to gain a clear view of our practices (including, but not restricted to, our linguistic practices), and of what these presuppose – *our 'engulfment' in 'the world'* or, more prosaically, our being a part of it, rather than either cultivating *or* directly countering a fantasized alienation from it.

Let me turn to the philosophers who were, I think, the first fully to recognize this: John *Dewey*, the greatest of the American Pragmatist philosophers, and, perhaps less directly but even more crucially because more 'diagnostically' effective, Ludwig *Wittgenstein*, the great linguistic 'philosopher'. Approaches to the question at hand, either taken directly or derived from their philosophizing, help us to abandon the linguistic practices that tend to perpetuate the Nature-vs-Culture problematic.

Dewey argued in various works that, if one were to talk about nature and culture at all, then cultures were best understood as, very roughly, 'special cases' of nature.[4] That is, he held human behaviour to be the most complex and rapidly evolving of all phenomena, but not qualitatively distinguishable from other animal behaviour.[5] Insofar as it could make sense to distinguish between cultures and 'the natural world' *at all*, then the distinction would be one of degree: more 'versus' less complex; and more 'versus' less malleable.

Thus if one wishes to talk, as philosophers and some others are strongly inclined to do, of Culture, or Nature, one should talk – one would be best advised so to talk, if one wishes to avoid potentially disabling philosophical (and ultimately political) confusions – roughly as follows: human cultures are communities of organisms that have reached a certain level of complexity and organization. They are not set against the natural (world) in the sense that there is some special feature unique to the human (Culture), which others (for example, 'primitive' humans, animals) lack. And one should emphasize that it is (overlapping) communities actively coping with the conditions that they meet that are engulfed in or a part of this world. This is crucial because one can then successfully evade the worry that in doing away with Nature vs Culture one is doing away with sociality altogether.

When one combines attention to Wittgenstein with this Deweyan perspective, a view of humans as *copers* with their context (including, crucially, their sociolinguistic surroundings), becomes more achievable still. And 'context' and 'surroundings' are *not*, in Wittgenstein, found in the misleading and potentially dangerous guise of either Nature *or* Culture. Rather, what Wittgenstein termed our 'forms of life'/'patterns of living' are *internally* related to ... 'the world'? Perhaps, but – perhaps better still – a word more appropriate for what we are necessarily, undifferentiatedly engulfed in, and engaged in, is ... our *environment(s)*. Wittgenstein held that each of the following three formulations amounts to much the same thing: that we judge similarly; that we share a pattern of living (or 'form of life'); and that we (in other words, any community of speakers/hearers/*copers*) simply *share a common environment* that we are always already a part of, an environment in which the 'cultural' elements and the 'natural' elements are *not qualitatively distinguishable*.

To see this, consider the following: what might cause one to believe that a group of animals has a culture? Possibly we would say that a bunch of dolphins or baboons held in cages 'under laboratory conditions' do not; but what would be the ground for saying this of such a bunch acting in a context that did not prevent their *inter*action? Only, I think, the reasonable presumption that by and large they don't have *language*.

This issues in the following: the 'linguistic' behaviour engaged in by non-human animals is not of sufficient complexity to earn the name of 'language'; but beyond this brute fact we have no reason for denying that non-human animals can have/can be part of culture, for some do have reproducible 'social systems' – one easily calls to mind images of gorillas or orangutans (or even otters) in their natural settings improvising tools, playing, showing affection for each other, communicating in various ways, and so on – of a kind that involve mutual engagement in and with their environment, an environment that they partially constitute and continually modify. But if this description is sound, then *on what principled basis* is the dividing line between culture and non-culture to be drawn?

In Dewey's works the very term *environment* is used in precisely the way indicated earlier, as marking and involving an *inextricability*, an utter impossibility of breaking apart what have been called cultural and natural elements. And while Wittgenstein's practice involved no such explicit use of the term, a conception of existence as active engagement, as a part(icipation) in a whole or wholes, is among the most crucial of his later philosophical insights. It is common ground between Wittgenstein and Dewey that the environment(s) of human animals are inextricably cultural/natural, and this is the locus of 'a connection of a man [sic], in the way of both dependence and support, with the enveloping world'.[6]

The advantages of the term *environment* begin with the observation that this term may have the capacity to displace *both culture* and *nature*. And we have now seen why such displacement is necessary; for if there is no opposition between the terms *nature* and *culture*, then there is no point in holding that 'everything is natural', or in finding nature to be normative. Ironically enough, Nature can neither be 'naturalized' (that is, taken to refer to some actually existing entity, by reduction or by some other theoretic means), nor usefully invoked in ethical discourse. The term *environment* can help us succeed where the dualistic terms have failed if we understand ourselves as already *part of* most environments that we describe. And if we understand *environment* not as a near-synonym for *nature*, talk of one's environment *need_not* be an attempt to *discriminate* between first nature, second nature and non-nature.

A further advantage of the term *environment*, then, is that its pluralization is much more straightforward than in the case of *nature* – it can make perfect sense to talk of environments of massively different scales and forms.

But there remains one simple but crucial problem: it is *still* just a little too easy to see one's *environment* as something *external* to one (compare the frequent use among [say] politicians of the phrase 'the natural environment' as a quasi-synonym for *nature*). There is a term available that circumvents this difficulty while retaining all the advantages of *environment* detailed earlier and remaining true to the insights of Wittgenstein and company: *ecosystem*. It is *built into* the concept that one cannot sustain an external perspective towards one's ecosystem(s). My proposal, my suggestion, then, comes down to this: that we try refraining completely from the vocabulary of nature and culture and instead work seriously and passionately with the vocabulary of different and in most cases of *preferable/less preferable ecosystem(s)*.

Imagine at this point the following objection: 'But then has anything been achieved? For everything will rest on who does the designating of "preferable" and "non preferable". And will there not run throughout either a deep anthropocentrism, by which any ecosystem in which life is more *comfortable* – or convenient, or "focused-upon the needs of", etc. – for humans (as opposed to other creatures, or even plants) will be deemed preferable to a "biocentrism" (in which the opposite is true)?'

The worry motivating the latter question simply *has no substance* unless one first sets up an antithesis of human vs nature – for, beyond this antithesis, humans (and also those organisms that humans have changed, introduced, and so on) are *part* of the 'bios' that one talks of centring. And the objector's first question *similarly* fails: it does not appreciate the point that we have *nowhere* to begin but with the reality of our inclusion in an ecological collective even as we think we experience things from without. Thus, exact identity of this 'we' will simply have to be contested, where it is contestable, through whatever sociopolitical channels are available. For instance, the inclusion of non-human animals in a 'we' will have to be attested to and contested, generally on a case-by-case basis. What I am suggesting here, and will further argue below, is that to focus on ecosystem(s) (including us) as a whole(s), to which we can (and inevitably will) make a difference, can be *empowering* and sanguine.

Specifically, once we are non-anthropocentric to the extent of saying that 'the value of natural objects and processes is not reducible to human interests or preferences', not to 'the value of the human experience or forms of consciousness excited by them',[7] then, 'environmental ethics is inescapably human-centred [only] in a way that blurs the distinction between purely "human" and purely "environmental" values'.[8] Exactly. Any more 'radical' effort at theorizing and practising a value-system 'independent' of humans founders on the incoherent notion of human animals judging and acting via criteria totally independent of themselves, as if magically written down somewhere or refereed by some ghostly official. What I am suggesting Wittgenstein and Dewey and their authentic successors in philosophy (and in political activism) suggest is the deflation of both Culture and Nature, *via* the suggestion that we think and talk instead simply in terms of (local, regional, global, and so on) ecosystem(s), and (of course) that we conceive of ourselves as part of those ecosystems, but not as incapable of making judgements about that which we co-constitute, not as having to judge and value totally without reference to ourselves, which would be logically impossible.

What I want now provisionally to suggest is that, though the rough-and-ready distinction between the *natural* and the *cultural* may stay in our ordinary language, we would do well to ignore or abjure it entirely when engaged in any form of 'theorizing', when reflecting with care upon our situation, and stick to talking of the environment(s), or (often much better) of the *ecosystem*(s), as approximately 'defined' earlier. For *natural* and *cultural* have turned out not to be terms that we can reliably *hang* anything on. (The terms *nature* and *culture*, as we have seen, are in fact just too prone to lead to philosophical trouble.)

Again, I have not argued for the elimination from our ordinary language of the terms *natural*, *man-made*, *cultural*, and so forth. After Wittgenstein, far be it from a philosopher to attempt to *legislate* language use. Mere language 'policemen' will never achieve anything of significance. Rather, I have tried to emphasize that *qua* 'theorists' – in as much as we are intellectuals, or thinkers, or reflective political actors – we would do well to notice something we often fail to appreciate and need (in Wittgenstein's sense) to be reminded of, namely that we are deeply – entirely – embedded in our ecosystem(s) prior to setting up the binary oppositions through which we structure many of our less immediately practical 'language-games', oppositions such as nature vs culture. We are 'thrown' into the world if you like – but from *within* it, as part of it – it makes no *sense* to think of us as opposed to it. As long as language is used, terms such as *nature*, *technology* and *human* will probably have a meaning, a use, but *that* doesn't imply that, *qua* 'theorists', and (even) when putting our 'theories' into action, we should use them. And that is all.[9]

We should, then, move on beyond romantic or 'deep' defences of nature, with their attendant structural dangers of valorizing 'the norm' in the same breath as 'the natural environment' is normatively affirmed (compare: 'heterosexual sex and reproduction is *natural*, is *normal*') and, of course, we simultaneously move beyond the reverse image (to the defence of Nature), the exploitation and domination of Nature. There can be no *pre*judgment either for or against technoscientific interventions in ecosystem(s): each case is to be judged on its merits, pragmatically.

'Is this not covertly to judge against the ecological stability and survival of the planet, for are we not all-too-familiar with technological reason blundering into an ecosystem (say, when jetties were constructed to stop beach erosion, only often to exacerbate the problem) under the masquerade of being value-free/neutral?'

These 'masquerades' should indeed be challenged, particularly in respect of the underlying complicity of 'free-market' ideology with the threats to and worsening of many of our ecosystems, but I think that the only prejudgement that can be made against techoscientific interventions is the very common-or-garden point that in general one shouldn't expend time and energy and precious resources on projects whose likely risk-laden effects one is deeply uncertain of, and so on. Such truisms are arguably all one can generate from an environmental ethic prior to getting one's hands 'dirty' with empirical details, normative commitments and hard decisions, unless one is prepared to endorse one of the extreme/incoherent perspectives criticized earlier. (Thus we can diagnose any alleged anti-anthropocentric biocentrism as among other things a perhaps-gendered attempt to escape from the 'dirty', 'messy' realities of living in a world, with others, committed to things, trying to make difficult decisions, sometimes making mistakes, and so on.) The hope must be that an *up-front emphasis on all aspects of our ecosystem(s)*, not just the 'natural' or the 'man-made', will enable us (at the margin) to make better ecological decisions. For by the time we are faced with trying to make an ethical/political choice between competing ecosystemic goods, it is already *too late* to turn to Nature as a final basis on which to decide. At the point of our making such choices the (alleged) naturalness of 'Nature' may even be quite beside the point. For again, Nature cannot be usefully naturalized/totalized/categorized any more than Reason can. Both are contested ideals.

The dysfunctional environmental practices of many, both locally and globally, should be even more obvious than they are at present if my proposal is acted upon, while there need be no knee-jerk reactions against technological means of improving our ecosystems. Consider the following point: is one really going to object to applying any technology whatsoever (provided such technology is itself not very harmful) to the pressing task of redressing what we judge to be harms done to our ecosystems (by, for instance, past techno-ecological catastrophes)? But then consider this: what principled grounds are there for distinguishing qualitatively between changes to an ecosystem amounting to a redress of past harms done to it, and changes constituting alterations of an ecosystem for the better, but where there is no redressing of any particular past harm? If one agrees with the arguments given in the present chapter, one will agree that this has become – *ceteris paribus* – a distinction without a (relevant) difference, and that it is possible to judge that a human-altered ecosystem is preferable to one in its natural state. (A possible example might be the English Lake District's 'improvement' by its partial deforestation and valley-floor draining a thousand years ago. The Lake District has arguably been beautified in a manner whose negative consequences for some flora and fauna are not overwhelming.)[10]

If one *disagrees*, one is left in the uncomfortable position of having to explain on a philosophical/theoretical basis why only *some* deliberately engineered alterations in the environment constitute harms, and which do; why in particular we did not 'let things take their natural course' (a telling phrase) after, for instance, Chernobyl, rather than send in damage-control teams and environmental clean-up crews. There is no road back from technology as such; any such road, even if we truly wished to take it (as surely no one who has really thought about it actually does), could only be a technological one.

There are only different technologies, and serious reasons for believing that *certain* technologies (nuclear and perhaps GM) must be abandoned or resisted. This is what I have been saying: that any general philosophico-theoretical naturalization of these hard decisions is untenable. We have to face up to being in a world where being Green is not simple. Yes, we should work to 'build down' our industrial society such that it is sustainable in the long term, such that we can sustain a culture semi-*permanently*,[11] but we should not be dogmatic about the methods we use to do this. Sometimes one does need to use the master's tools to rebuild the master's house.

To recap: I contend that the cash-value of looking at questions of how to organize our activities in the world in the fashion that I am suggesting is twofold:

1). Extreme views may get ruled out as just obviously inadequate, because they incoherently fail even rudimentarily to observe our ecological interdependence. (To give another example: most – cynical – 'wise use' advocates, who seem actually just to be covering for the worsening of some beautiful and rich lands in the cause of short-term economic growth.)

2). We are forced to address more directly and less obfuscatorily reasons for one course of action or another. We have to explain how some action will improve the ecosystem in question (in terms of aesthetics, sustainability, and so on), and enhance the lives of those we take to be of relevance. Quality of environment(s) is increasingly a major factor in how citizens of the contemporary West are prepared to structure their life-choices; a democratic faith would enjoin us to frame ecological questions in a manner resembling the one that I am proposing, and would not require that citizens be regaled with overarching reasons for exploiting or for defending Nature. I would argue that it is education, mass activism and a mass challenge to the so-called 'economic imperatives' shaping our ecosystems right now that are required, not new theories of nature or the rights of Nature (or, indeed, even of Culture). If we are 'required', for the sake of short-term eco-political goals, to speak with the Naturalists, to speak of 'despoiling/ wounding Nature', then so be it. But to paraphrase Richard Rorty (on feminism), although this may be so, Greens would profit from at least *thinking* (and, insofar as one does so at all, theorizing) with the Pragmatist-Wittgensteinians.

Of course, point 2 above will not settle questions *a priori*; the core of my proposal is terminological, not substantively ethical. Terms such as 'ecosystem' and 'community' will remain contested. But at least they promise not to be irremediably confused or confusing, and at least they bring with them relatively few of the risks of the rhetoric of Nature (and Culture) identified above.

And so: there has been no effort here to seek to *regain* an original and allegedly lost unity (with the planet); only to find ways of understanding just how a certain unity of all part(icipant)s in the ecosystem(s) has *never* been threatened (because conceptually it *cannot* be threatened), has always been available to us. Literary theorists, feminists, life-scientists and eco-activists need not be threatened by the argument of this chapter; what has been proposed is simply that we 'clarify' what we are doing when we 'theorize' about ecology. I don't believe that philosophy can dictate to one one's ethical commitments and political actions; but philosophy can help us to gain a clear view of what we are *already* in one way or another committed to.

I do not intend, then, to have outlined a hubristic general political strategy here, nor even to have protested against many of the ideas and rallying calls of environmentalists. Instead, it should be clear that I too love and value 'wild nature'. I love and value much old (as well as some new) wilderness. I would like to see a Buffalo Commons in the plains of the USA, and wolves back in Scotland. I just don't think that philosophy or any form of theorizing can *instruct* us that we ought to have a Buffalo Commons or wolves back in Scotland. Philosophy 'leaves these things as they are', but, at its best, gives us a much better *opportunity* for changing ourselves, and them … in fact, for creating, anew, rather than merely returning to an (often fantasized) past. The centre of my philosophical point has been this: that a philosophical anti-anthropocentrism is nonsensical, and that a philosophical 'foundation' for green practice is not required. We can advocate a Buffalo Commons without imagining, absurdly, that we are literally going 'back to nature'.

A final possible 'epigraph' possibly suggests itself, then:

Neither Nature, nor Culture, but forward to (international) ecologism …

For the sake of the avoidance of conceptual confusion and of needless endless discussion, and for the sake of what we are already often happy enough to call 'the environment', let us consider not the construction of Nature by Culture or vice versa, but rather simply *what ecosystem(s) we wish to live in and to secure for future inhabitants of this ecosystem/of this planet* and how to achieve these goals. That is, through both the requisite use of 'linguistic practices' (such as this chapter hopes in its small way to be) and of 'non-linguistic practices' (changing our eating habits, producing genuinely ecological art, boycotting the shares of the nuclear industry and of other Greenpeace targets, 'monkey-wrenching' if and when and where necessary ...).

I have suggested, controversially, that Dewey and Wittgenstein are in the end philosophers of and for the green movement. And that movement is a movement whose time, it is now increasingly obvious to everyone, has truly come. What the greens have been warning of for a generation is coming tragically true. Our societies must change direction now, before it is too late, listening to those who were and remain the visionaries: the greens, the ecologists.

And, starting from philosophical reflection, what are the greens saying?:

We are *part* of our ecosystem. We are one with it. We are *nothing* without it. We cannot successfully conceptualize ourselves at all without thinking of ourselves as part of the Earth. The environment, properly speaking, is not something else. Nature is not something else. It is us, and we are it.

The term *ecosystem* is best placed to bring these reminders into prominence. Suitably reminded, let us get busy in defence of a viable ecosphere. Let us bring into lived reality the convenient truth that a world in which we radically reduce our CO_2 emissions by scaling down and re-localizing our lives will be a *happier* world. And let us always bear in mind a question that one day we may well be asked quite directly: 'Mum, Dad: what did YOU do, to help save the future? ...'

2 The Cost of Growth: Climate *Change*, *Crisis* and *Chaos*

This chapter is about consequences

The previous chapter, 'We Are Part of Our Ecosystem', explored the problematic 'Culture vs Nature' dichotomy. The way out of the trouble this view of things – this dichotomy – prompted was the realization of another option: *ecosystem*, which more accurately captures the complex relationship between humans and the natural world: humans are *part of* this world, not 'external' to it in the way that the word 'environment' can too easily imply. In this way, Chapter 1 provided a key example of philosophy serving as 'therapeutic' action. The 'therapy' I proposed forces the old dichotomies to loosen their grip on our thinking and helps to establish the relatively new, vital concept of ecosystem (and of ecosystemic thinking) in a central place in our minds, our lives, our actions.

The present chapter builds upon the analysis of nature and ecosystem just described. I will demonstrate here how therapeutic philosophy further grounds the notion of philosophy (as) applied in action, and makes the case for a centrality of politics in such an endeavour. I argue here that the advent of man-made dangerous climate change requires a new philosophy, a philosophical response which must begin with a careful look at our practices.

And I hope to have begun that new looking through the perspective shift exemplified above – by getting us to see that our problems are not perhaps as separate from one another as we want them to be. There is a holistic aspect to the difficulties and philosophical challenge of our current world situation. Carnage on our roads, carnage in the Middle East and the slow carnage of anthropogenic climate change – these are simply three sides of the same coin. (As in medicine, doctors sometimes speak of pills having certain 'side effects'. But there is no such thing as '*side* effects'. There are only *effects* ...)

*   *   *

As I write, in November 2006, the Republicans have at last lost control of the United States Congress. In part, this is because virtually no one now believes the lies of the spin-saturated governments of the USA and the UK: the biggest lie of all is that the war on Iraq had nothing to do with oil. The truth is that, worried about the stability of the Saudi regime and worried about the independence of the Islamist Iranian government, Bush-Blair wanted to get their dirty, and now bloody, hands on the vast oil reserves of Iraq, which were of course in the grip of the bloody and, far more importantly from Washington's point of view, worryingly independent Saddam regime.

The West invaded Iraq so that western businesses might control the oil fields there. The west props up Israel so that it has a reliable strong-man in the Middle East. Every time we fill up with petrol, and choose to risk car-nage on the roads of Britain or America, we also choose to fuel longer-term carnage on the streets of Gaza and Baghdad and Jerusalem.

Oil and petrol; cars and killers. It's time to start thinking seriously about the connections here. And the consequences.

There's death over there and there's (some) death over here, and it's all tragic. But it is also predictable. The predictable consequence of sacrificing whatever it takes to provide ourselves with the resources to fuel economic growth. To move people and stuff around faster and faster, to increase economic throughput. Carnage is the terrible, horrible, sad consequence of growth, of attempting 'to give my children more than I had'. And this must be accepted, because, we tell ourselves, growth is a positive thing. Perhaps the MOST positive thing ...

But picture the following:

- A child who grows to be 1 metre tall. Then 2 metres. Then 4 metres. Then 8 metres … That's growth!
- A child who becomes better and better at maths, or at running, or at understanding other people. That's development.
- A cancer or a parasite that spreads – until it overwhelms the organism which it inhabits. That's growth!
- A cancer that is treated; and an organism that finds ways of living which make it is less likely to contract cancer again. That's development.

Today, as 2006 comes to an end, humanity is burning fossil fuels *like there's no tomorrow*. We are told that this is essential for economic growth.

And surely everyone agrees that economic growth at least is a good thing … Don't they?

* * *

The burning of fossil fuels – the very thing that is driving our growth – in record quantities is producing pollution (especially, 'greenhouse' gases such as CO_2) in record quantities. As our economy grows, the remaining capacity of our environment to absorb these wastes shrinks. Can we *afford* this growth, if we start thinking long-term? If we think like there's always – or *should* be, always – a tomorrow, for us and for our children?

My own response to this question brings home to me that growth just isn't necessarily a good thing. It's a means to an end, at best. The real goal is the satisfaction of needs and a worthwhile existence. So when growth *doesn't* lead to needs being satisfied, and doesn't contribute to a meaningful life for all, it should be stopped. We should stop growth – the way we seek instantly to stop the growth of cancer – that is not helping us to be happier, not merely because such growth can't go on indefinitely anyway, but because it is *pointless*.

A world in which our use of resources (and our wasting them) spreads until it finally overwhelms the life-supporting capacity of the planet itself. That's growth – to the point of collapse. For example, Christian Aid (n.d.) recently released the results of a study indicating that up to 180 million people in Africa alone are likely to die unnecessary deaths as a result of the impact of unmitigated climate change before the twenty-first century comes to an end. If we do not stop that horrific prediction from coming true, that will be the equivalent of one man-made climate-change Hiroshima every fortnight. That's (the cost of) growth. That's the reason why the greatest green-leaning philosopher of economics, Herman Daly, has said that we must move *beyond* growth in our thinking and our actions.

This is the legacy that we may very well hand to our children if we do not begin, right now, to conceive of growth differently, and not necessarily to value it.

Liberal political philosophy, the philosophy (of men such as John Locke and John Rawls) that has underpinned the 'liberal democracies' such as Britain and the USA from the Enlightenment on, argues that there must be some sense in which 'all men are created equal', and that beyond that sense people must be free to do what they want, including building up their own wealth. This has been the engine for economic growth. But our time is a time when such growth is no longer a good thing. Liberal political philosophy has helped to *create* the long emergency that is man-made climate change. To escape from that emergency, we need a *different* philosophy. A philosophy for climate change. A philosophy of sustainability. And indefinitely-prolonged growth *cannot possibly* be sustainable. You can only sustain indefinitely an economy that stops growing, that stops creating ever-heavier demands on the ecosystem within which it subsists. 'Economic growth' really means: ever-increasing throughput of materials. That is unsustainable.

* * *

Yet still some argue – echoing a major tenet of western philosophy since at least Francis Bacon – 'isn't growth *itself* the solution to the problem of growth?' Hasn't the unprecedented growth we've experienced in recent years reaped fruits, or rather powered the reaping of fruits, that will furnish us with the ability to overcome the problem posed by growth? If we work and think hard, for instance, can't we find ways to still have growth and yet avoid climate catastrophe – like new technologies? What about feeding our need for growth with other, less harmful fuel sources – hasn't this already spurred on the search for alternative energy?

'Peak Oil' is all set to make it even harder to prevent the degradation of human civilization within a century that catastrophic climate change would mean – melting the ice-caps, flooding our coasts and cities, burning the Amazon, creating hundreds of millions of environmental refugees, rendering large parts of the Earth simply uninhabitable, bringing hurricanes even to England. Why? Because, as oil starts running out, unless we are very well prepared, the first effect will be massive economic downturns and instabilities. Remember the 'oil shocks' of the 1970s? You ain't seen nothin' yet compared to the oil shocks that Peak Oil threatens us with. Major economic instability will make it far harder to find the absolutely essential political will to change our economy to a low-carbon economy.

Even more worryingly, as the oil fields of Kuwait and Saudi Arabia go into decline, attention will shift to the lower-quality bitumen, tar and 'heavy oil' supplies found in countries such as Canada and Venezuela. The problem with these is that they require far more energy to extract than do existing oil fields. How do you get that energy? Most likely by burning oil (or gas, or coal) ...

You see the problem: as we scramble to find replacements for our dwindling oil supplies, we will burn much more fossil fuel in order to get hold of new supplies. That means more carbon emissions. Some kinds of coal have CO_2 emissions forty times as high as those from conventional oil. If we start burning that coal, we really are signing humanity's suicide note.

We must not do so. We must not kill the future. So: what we have to do is plan NOW to avoid jumping from the frying pan of Peak Oil into the furnace of global overheat. We have to move fast to transform our lives. And so maybe Peak Oil and even potentially-catastrophic climate change are good news in the end. Maybe this 'overgrowth' may prompt us to make the changes in our lives, in our society, that we need to make anyway ... ?

Maybe not. According to *The New York Times*, for instance, 'research into energy technologies by both government and industry has not been rising, but rather falling'.[1] In fact the only alternative energy source that's been given serious consideration is nuclear power. Remember nuclear power – the 'safe' alternative to fossil fuels which we were told (by Ronald Reagan, for instance) would produce so little waste that it could fit beneath a desk? Remember 3-Mile Island? Remember Chernobyl?

Here's the legacy we are handing to our children. Nuclear power is supposed to allow continual economic business as usual; forget global overheating, forget Peak Oil: yes, here's the growth we can safely pursue ...

Right? ...

The British and American governments tell us they want to achieve 'energy security'. This counts against resources – such as oil, gas *and uranium* – which come mostly from countries which are politically insecure. Furthermore, nuclear is much more vulnerable and deadly than these fossil fuels (which in turn are much more vulnerable and deadly than renewables: you can't really imagine terrorists bothering to fly a plane into a wind-farm or a tidal barrage, let alone into mini-wind turbines and solar panels on people's houses ... Note that, if a plane were flown into a nuclear reactor, its pilots wouldn't have even needed to have got hold of any nuclear material in order to unleash a truly unprecedented catastrophe).

So I wonder: would a terrorist prefer us to depend on a few centralized nuclear power stations, or on millions of micro-generation systems for individual homes or communities, when it comes to the security of a network? And which would the terrorists stipulate when it came to potential targets for explosions? Nuclear waste stockpiles (and the REALLY BIG desk we must be putting them under!) and nuclear power stations? Or factories making wind turbines and warehouses full of insulation materials?

Now, a society based on lower levels of energy – but safe renewable energy – a society in which people are doing less, slower, but what they are doing is increasingly satisfying to them; a society in which people's real needs are satisfied ... *that's development*, and *development*, in its true sense, is always a good thing. We are all, I hope, part of the developing world in this sense ...

An important philosophic conclusion: it is quality of life, not mere material standard of living, that matters. Liberal political philosophers argue that we must not discriminate against individuals' choices as to how to live their lives; so it underwrites improvements in 'standard of living', but suggests that there can be no sound basis for discriminating objectively between different types of life. I disagree. I submit that pursuit of a higher material standard of living – via 'growth' – is worsening everybody's quality of life, even that of the rich, for the rich too are suffering a spiritual poverty and a growing sense of insecurity and a worsening natural environment.

The era of 'Peak Oil' and 'Climate Chaos' is an era in which the political philosophy that has dominated our time, and that has set the parameters for economic neo-liberalism the world over, has thoroughly outlived its usefulness. Now is the time not for liberalism but for a sustainable philosophy of the future. Now is the time for a green radicalism.

*   *   *

From the point of view outlined above, growth certainly has a severe downside, but it could still be seen by some as tangential; i.e. it's how we have *managed* growth that is harmful, it might be said. But when one thinks about it further, (economic) growth really isn't all it's cracked up to be anyway. Sure, an economy in which *more* and *more* people are rushing around ever faster clocking up *more* wages (and *more and more* debts!), but not feeling *any more* happy at the end of the day: that's also growth. Together with our reckless abuse of fossil fuel resources, one can see a symptomatology which reveals that the consequences of our growth addiction, our oil and energy addiction are symptoms of a bigger problem ...

We should note that, in the short to medium term, there is *no* prospect of achieving carbon emissions reduction without reduction in demand for transport, industrial production, and so on. (This is why the fixation on technology – as a solvent to dangerous climate change – of all the G8 countries is so depressing; it alone cannot possibly reduce emissions sufficiently *now*; and the climate scientists tell us we may have as little as ten years to stabilize the climate.) But my scepticism as to the prospect of 'smart' low-carbon growth is *not* based principally on scepticism as to the viability of genuinely renewable energy (i.e. on alternatives to fossil fuels *and* to unsustainable nuclear fuels, which, just like fossil fuels, are finite and generate unacceptable levels of pollution). For while I think that a transition to a renewables-based economy will be painful, and will involve some severe shocks for the world's economy, and while I am certain that emissions must be reduced now through demand-reduction, I think it is clear that a renewables-based world economy *can* eventually be achieved. Recent research by the Oxford University Environmental Change Institute[2] indicates that a well-balanced 'shopping basket' of renewables, coming on and off stream to different degrees at different times of the day and night throughout the year could potentially provide us with much of what we 'need' in Britain within a generation – and with *all* of what we need *if we build down our energy use*, full stop, very substantially, over the coming generation.

So my scepticism is not based principally on any doubts I might have about the (medium–long term) prospects for renewable energy. For let us imagine for a moment what would, so many intelligent people might think, be the very *best* that we can hope for. Let us imagine that the continuing increase in carbon emissions across the planet, which is currently terrifying scientists and blighting humanity's future, *is* reversed, via a *temporary* contraction of our energy use, *prior to* the achievement of the dream of *very plentiful* supplies of renewables being realized. Let us imagine that we do then drastically build up our energy use and our economic activity *once* we have found climate-friendly ways of doing so. Let us imagine that effective renewable sources are quickly and hugely harnessed; what then?

Imagine it: imagine the nightmare that would actually result. Imagine cars free to clog up our streets to their owners content, if they all ran on cheap renewable energy. Imagine our skies filled with the noise of aeroplanes running perhaps on biofuel or solar batteries. Imagine the factories that would spring into overdrive, using this ultra-cheap harmless energy to produce all manner of goods that we don't really need or want – far more than we already have (far more cars and planes, far more throw-away goods ...).

And then imagine the new crises that would surely, rapidly follow. Imagine raw materials running out one after another, as corporations use them up helter-skelter to create huge profits, using the renewable energy that would perhaps be 'too cheap to metre'. Imagine our waste dumps overflowing – far worse than they already do. Imagine doses of the synthetic materials that are poisoning our environment multiplying exponentially. Imagine the epidemics of cancer. Imagine the species destroyed by the rush to mine and build on places previously too costly, energy-wise, to do so. Imagine the vast degradation of the world's soil, as intensive farming is unshackled from the costs of energy and yields are pumped up for agribusiness's sake ...

A world whose limited capacities to provide us with resources and to absorb our pollution we *recognize*, and live within. That would be true development. Such recognition, such 'living lightly on the Earth', would show that the human race had *really* learned, *really* developed, *really* made progress. Wouldn't this be a great legacy to give to our children?

But, in reality, that world is quite a way away. Therefore, the legacy that *we* must hand to *our* children (and, certainly, encourage them to hand another, better legacy onto theirs) is one of dogged effort and (finally) foresight. It is a legacy of change and a willingness to think and act (and consume) differently than we have before. And that legacy is at hand. In the early stages of the worldwide growth crisis, a remarkably effective potential worldwide solution has been presented by Aubrey Meyer's Global Commons Institute.[3] It is called 'Contraction and Convergence': contraction of CO_2 emissions, to a scientifically-agreed safe level, and convergence of emissions towards the same per capita status, worldwide.

'Contraction and convergence', first for carbon, and later for raw materials and some other pollutants too, to prevent subsequent possible crises, is a suitable philosophy for the era in which economic growth threatens to create catastrophe. C&C has what is required to face the global growth crisis primarily because it is acceptable to anyone who thinks carefully enough about the 'arguments' and rhetoric that have heretofore been used to stall such greening. In other words, it is equitable: it is put forward on the basis of the right of each individual to an equal entitlement of the maximum amount of carbon emissions that is consistent with climate safety for all, including for those as yet unborn. It would ensure human survival because it will be based on the best climate science in drawing up safe emissions levels. Actually, it will be equitable *because* it will lead to human survival: insufficiently radical action to counter the threat of climate chaos imposes grossly unfair burdens on those whose lives are threatened by that chaos; especially our children. And it will lead to human survival *because* it is equitable: any other deal will be unacceptable either to developed nations (which will ask why they should constrain their own CO_2 emissions, if developing nations are not bound to) or to developing nations (which will ask why they should be forbidden development when it is developed nations that have damaged the world's climate and reaped the economic benefits of having done so).

Something we can all agree on: what a *development*!

This, I believe, *is* the philosophy of climate change that I have been in search of in this chapter: equal rights in the true 'commons' of our world, such as the atmosphere. Such that these commons should never be privatized; they are held in trust by us for each other and for future generations. Future generations, which are never taken seriously in liberal political philosophies, must be at the heart of our thinking now. A radical green philosophy for the future argues for use – not ownership – by all, including those as yet unborn, of the world's greatest riches. Of what makes life possible: the 'services' provided for free by our ecosystem, such as screening out the harmful UV rays of the sun (via the ozone layer) and coping with the greenhouse gas emissions that we have been too profligately pumping into the skies.

So it is clear: we must adopt Contraction and Convergence and save the world ... well, yes, of course we must. But I think there is one other thing that needs to be considered. Despite all of its promising features, Contraction and Convergence *just won't work* – it won't be *sustained* – unless we enter into it having thoroughly broken our growth addiction. Relying on technology to improve energy efficiency measures and on alternative fuels to power our lifestyles is good, but ultimately a 'co-dependent' of the absolute conviction held by many that growth is unmitigatedly good and that once one has more, there is no turning back to less. The problem is that until we have conquered the disease, we can at best only control the symptoms. Consider one example:

A major goal for reducing vehicular pollution is to move to low-emissions vehicles.[4] The European Union has target emissions levels, agreed by heads of states and governments, to reach an average CO_2 emission figure of 120 gms/km for all new passenger cars by 2010. Yet it was reported in April 2006 that 2005 saw only a 1 per cent decrease to an average of 160 gms CO_2 per km. This is a failure in responsibility by car manufacturers, and a break of the promise that their industry group, the European Automobile Manufacturers Association (ACEA), made back in 1998 when they promised the European Commission to reach average emissions of 140 gms CO_2 per km for new cars by 2008. But that promise can only be a first step, a transition, a sort of economic methadone that we take to overcome our much more powerful, much uglier addiction.

The strongest, more completely effective method we may employ to yet save our beautiful blue-green planet, however, includes ultimately switching (gradually, eventually) to 'feet first' transport methods – walking and cycling – and to other low-impact means of getting about. By working from home and communicating with people the smart way, by phone and computer, and soon by video phoning and ultra-cheap internet videoconferencing.

That will be a really happy day for the Earth, for our

children and for billions of non-human creatures: when we humans turn decisively towards ways of moving, and ways of being, that can last. When we cure our 'affluenza'. And such a cure must be real, not merely a superficial gesture.

Consider the new trend in travel, a new 'ethical' fashion afoot. It is called 'carbon offsetting'. Many of the big rock bands are doing it – for example, Pearl Jam, Coldplay and the Rolling Stones. Carbon offsetting means taking actions such as planting trees in order to compensate for the damage that one does by burning fossil fuels, by flying, for instance. The coming of carbon offsetting is surely a welcome development, inasmuch as it shows that an increasing number of people are trying to 'offset' the damage that they do to our planetary life-support system. But how effective is it?

The first point to make is that even in the best case scenario, carbon offsetting only neutralizes damage that one is actually doing. It is not a positively good thing; it is not like giving to a worthwhile charitable or political cause, for instance, that will actually change the world for the better. It is only making up for real harm that one has done, by (say) dumping several tons of carbon in the atmosphere by taking a plane. Furthermore, if the money that one spends on carbon offsetting is money that one would otherwise have spent on other worthwhile activities that would reduce one's carbon footprint, then it may be no good *at all*. If I can only afford to offset my carbon emissions by reducing the amount that I spend on local organic produce, for instance, then there is *no* genuine carbon offset effect.

If we are to avert climate catastrophe, if we mean to hand the legacy of change to the next generation, it will require great effort – perhaps a greater effort than any that has preceded it – to break our addiction to growth. But this does not mean that the daunting news of global crisis and the mounting possibility of subsequent international chaos should reduce us to utter despair, or paralyse us with inaction. We know what to do. We have done it before. It is part of who we are.

Remember the spirit of the Blitz: all of us pulling together, even when it involved sacrifices such as food rationing. People grumbled about food rationing during the Second World War sometimes, but by and large it worked and was adhered to. The long emergency that we are now entering requires similar sacrifices: for instance, signing up at the 'Flight Pledge' website,[5] and joining the new conscientious objectors: those who refuse to fly for pleasure and keep their flying to an absolute minimum.

Carbon offsetting is potentially good, but we need to and can do much better. Contraction and convergence will lead to genuine *carbon rationing*: each person should have a carbon ration that is worked out in such a way that the total of all the rations adds up to an amount that the climate can cope with. And if more carbon is 'spent' in one place, less must be 'spent' in another. But we can do even better still: by embracing an industrial build-down, by getting 'off the grid' whenever possible. By deciding to spend the energy and manage the inconvenience of carrying around a mug instead of relying on disposable cups for coffee and tea, even if the energy-intensive industrial processes that produce them are improved to maximum efficiency. Not solely by unplugging our wasteful appliances, which consume a high percentage of their operational energy just sitting idle, but by watching and being organized around less television. By taking an extra hour to trim the lawn with old-fashioned, manually rotating blade mowers (which worked well enough, didn't they?) rather than buying an electric lawn mower (even if you were doing the latter because you wanted to be more environmentally sound than you would be if you used your petrol-powered ride-on). By wearing a sweater in the winter, even inside your house. By ...

Perhaps we can dare to hope, having all learned from the experience of global warming-fed Hurricane Katrina, that even the USA might finally start to move faster towards real action to combat climate change. Such an intelligent response to such a disastrous change in the weather would at least give the many thousands of victims of this and other such hurricanes a kind of legacy. We *must* begin to act to prevent future destruction on such a scale, by tackling the causes of climate change. The unprecedented (for the USA) scale of the disaster that hit New Orleans in 2005 should already have made it quite clear that this isn't some academic debate. And it isn't just about people far away of whom we know little. Nor is this even just about, as I have relied upon so heavily above, our children and grandchildren. Unless we move now to curb carbon emissions drastically, worldwide, then, next time, it might be *us*. I hope people are ready to listen: we need something of the spirit of the Blitz here. We can only resolve the climate crisis if we all pull together.

The human race will have *grown up*, when we turn decisively, *collectively*, to implementing the policies that are needed to resolve the climate crisis, and to stop climate chaos from engulfing all that we hold dear. This again requires a decisive step beyond the excessive valorization of individual freedom that one finds in liberal political philosophy, which too often is little more than a consumerism applied to politics (think of Tony Blair's tedious and endless invocations of the value of 'choice'). And it is consumerism that has got us into these desperate straits ... We have to think of ourselves as a collective. We have to think of ourselves as a species. We will not survive unless we do so. 'Carbon offsetting' is an essentially individualist, quasi-charity-ist mode of response to the climate crisis. Such a response, laudable though it might be, is entirely insufficient. There is something more important than becoming one of the new conscientious objectors, who refuse to fly any more, or than becoming a conscientious and meticulous carbon offsetter: namely, working on a collective basis to achieve the policies (in the first instance, contraction and convergence and carbon rationing) that will lead to a true philosophy of climate change. That means *concerted* political action. If you are impressed by what I have argued in this chapter, then please give up flying, or at least take up carbon offsetting. But more important than either of those: put your money and your time into getting people elected who will ensure that before long we all do these things. For in the end this is a matter of all, or nothing at all. If by cycling more all I do is to free up more road space for roadhogs, or if by flying less all I do is to encourage airlines to recruit thoughtless others who can do more flying, than I have achieved very little. A philosophy of climate change must be a collectivist philosophy (if the word hadn't been so abused, I would say: a socialist philosophy. Socialist in a deeper sense than that envisaged by the great philosophers of socialism, such as Marx and Engels, who did not have clearly in view the *limits* of growth). We must act together, to ensure that as a whole we take the actions necessary to save the future.

Philosophers have a moral responsibility, at this crucial juncture, to stand up and be counted.[6] To make clear that justice for future generations demands the kind of actions that I have outlined in this chapter. Above all, I have argued that the climate crisis requires us to *ration equally* all those goods which can lead to catastrophic pollution or shortages. This is a distinctive philosophical answer to a desperate problem. A political philosophy of justice for all, including the future ones, requires this new principle – equality of ration – to replace the 'liberal' principles that have got us into this mess of climate chaos in the first place ...[7]

II Religion

Editor's Introduction

You can challenge someone's actions, and upset them. There are hurt feelings, or perhaps more. Challenge someone's beliefs (often achieved by challenging actions), and you upset him as well – but in a different and perhaps more deeply felt sense. This challenge, one might think, shoots straight to the core, to the bedrock upon which one's feelings about herself, one's relationships, one's *whole life* is built. (Too often, philosophy is scared to do just this, to challenge deeply. Look at how anodyne most discussions of 'medical ethics' or 'legal ethics' are. Philosophers should be willing to challenge, for instance, the assumption that the law is something that can be bought and sold – through buying the services of lawyers; 'legal ethics' stops at questions such as whether it is reasonable for a lawyer to enter a 'not guilty' plea for a client whom he knows is guilty). We generally take beliefs to be something greater, something deeper and more meaningful than actions.

This section challenges actions and beliefs, often by placing the two in juxtaposition with each other. Chapter 3, a longer and more philosophically rich extension of an essay previously published in *Quaker Religious Thought*, does this in a novel way (sure to upset the beliefs of at least some). It asks a question, 'Need we have any (religious) beliefs at all, to be religious?', and in so doing proposes that actions assume a 'dominant' position. Belief is the shadow of action, or, more dangerously, the shadow of inaction. In other words, *when you want to know what someone believes, what better place to look than at her actions*?

We believe certain things about life, ascribe certain values to it: it is better to be happy than sad, say, or comfortable rather than in pain. Many believe certain things about death: it is a path to some sort of bliss or torment, perhaps. If our beliefs are firm enough, there will likely follow actions: the actions taken by one trying to end her life either through suicide or euthanasia, for instance. One thinks of countless religious zealots who have ended their lives or have let it end (or facilitated its ending). But what is the case of our beliefs when there is no action – what of Hamlet who famously couldn't decide whether to be or not to be, or whether to 'rest' or 'sleep'? Chapter 4 explores belief from this vantage point. It invites the reader to try to decide whether 'death' or 'dying' is what they find aversive about mortality. Perhaps inaction, an inability to decide which course to follow, suggests that there is something incoherent in our beliefs. Perhaps Hamlet's fear had more to do with the possibility that his beliefs were somehow incoherent, ill thought through, than with the fact that he couldn't choose what to do.

Chapter 5 is a composite of selections from two essays on forgiveness, one published in *Reason Papers* and the other in *Literature and Philosophy: A Guide to Contemporary Debates* (New York: Palgrave, 2006). It seeks an inlet to these issues interesting in a similar way to its predecessor – what if, instead of having no action to match a supposed belief, there is an action that we all know of, but about which we do not know what to believe? We still get a primacy of action; in fact, we see how a seemingly simple action can be elevated to the level of a 'miracle': we know it happens, we see it happen, and yet we don't understand why, or *how*. Perhaps more importantly, however, this chapter also attests that 'beliefs' do not always follow from actions – if someone is forced to apologize to me, should I take that seriously?

Enter with belief, leave with action – that could be the motto of this section. In each of three ways, the author makes the suggestion that religion is not a name we give to beliefs. Instead, he suggests that it is the name for what we do (with or without beliefs). This fully realizes the communal aspect of religion – its being something we do with others – while stressing its deeply personal nature: it is MY actions that I am responsible for, that make me who I am. This multi-valanced thing has no substitute. There is no doctrine, no theory we can have to exempt us from our personal responsibility to see our 'belief's manifested in the world, from struggling to see them practised in (and by) ourselves each day.

3 Religion Without Belief: The Example of Quakerism's Political 'Consequences'[1]

The effect of making men think in accordance with dogmas, perhaps in the form of certain graphic propositions, will be very peculiar: I am not thinking of these dogmas as determining men's opinions but rather as completely controlling the expression of all opinions. People will live under an absolute, palpable tyranny, though without being able to say they are not free ... For dogma is expressed in the form of an assertion, and is unshakeable, but at the same time any practical opinion can be made to harmonize with it; admittedly more easily in some cases than in others. It is not a wall setting limits to what can be believed, but more like a brake which, however, practically serves the same purpose; it's almost as though someone were to attach a weight to your foot to restrict your freedom of movement. This is how dogma becomes irrefutable and beyond the reach of attack.

– Wittgenstein[2]

In today's America, neo-conservatives generate brutish policies for which liberals provide the ethical fig-leaf. There really is no other difference between them.

– Tony Judt[3]

It is often said nowadays that the question of how we can preserve a 'liberal' tolerant society in the face of so-called religious fundamentalism is an absolutely fundamental question for the western democracies. But despite frequent recent framing by (predominantly) western powers such as the USA and the UK, of a great war for society being waged between (religious, but most conspicuously) Islamic fundamentalism and Liberal democracy,[4] my suspicion is that the attitude of liberals towards religion – found in highly focused form in the work of the greatest theoretician of liberalism, the American political philosopher John Rawls – is now a *cause of* rather than a palliative for the 'clash of fundamentalisms' in the world today. I believe liberalism to be fundamentally intolerant of real religion, or true spirituality; I believe that this foments certain worrying currents of violent sedition at large in the world today; and I suggest that certain other seditious and non-seditious currents of religious (and non-religious) thought and action offer a resolution, a way out of the cul-de-sac of liberal political philosophy.

Liberalism claims to be tolerant of religion. But the central *problem* that emerges with the (Rawls's) 'Liberal' undertaking is this: how is it possible for those affirming a religious doctrine to take seriously their right to uphold that doctrine, if they are deemed unreasonable as soon as they try actually to *do* anything that will directly affect an extant regime or its policies? How can they be expected to treat as just a regime that will oppress them as soon as they threaten its 'impartiality'[5] between conceptions of the good?

* * *

Here is what Rawls states about what he has achieved, in 'The idea of public reason revisited':

> Throughout, I have been concerned with a torturing question in the contemporary world, namely: Can democracy and com-prehensive doctrines, religious or non-religious, be compatible? And if so, how? At the moment a number of conflicts between religion and democracy raise this question. [Public reason] *does not trespass upon religious beliefs and injunctions insofar as these are consistent with the essential constitutional liberties, including the freedom of religion and liberty of conscience.* There is, or need be, no war between religion and democracy.[6]

That all sounds very nice. But my claim is that political liberalism refuses point-blank ever to engage in serious debate with religion. It considers it of no consequence, and this is a potentially fatal insult: a religion can bear being hated; it cannot bear being deflated into a matter of merely ceremonial interest, with no ringing meaning for all, no existential or ethical depth, no consequential action-oriented message. And religion that liberalism permits is not allowed to trespass on 'essential constitutional liberties', such as the freedom of a state to force its citizens to fight for it, and the freedom of children from any form of state-sponsored proselytizing, even, for example, encouraging a primary school class to care passionately for their planet (on which, more below).

Political liberalism insists that religion be 'translated' into the thin discourse of 'public reason' for it to *be* of any consequence at all. 'Political liberalism' *nihilates* religion: all that it is prepared to call 'reasonable' religion is mere ceremony; *and all that it is prepared to call 'unreasonable' it is quite prepared ruthlessly to suppress* the moment it shows any sign of threatening the neutrality (let alone the power or stability) of the liberal state or 'civil society'. In effect, Political Liberalists consider religion that will not allow itself to be entirely *neutered* to be *seditious*.

I suspect that some readers may at this point be thinking, roughly, 'This is all very well, but the bottom line is that religion *is* dangerous. When religious believers act on their beliefs, they generally do bad things. Look at those Christians who want to murder abortionists in America; or look at those Muslims who want to murder Americans; religions must be brought to heel, and brought to respect the rules of a society that is not any longer founded on their precepts. Religion *is* inherently seditious, if it does not allow the liberal state to set limits to its powers and respect those limits'. To think along these lines is to think *precisely in the manner that Rawls encourages*. Looking carefully, however, it becomes transparent that Rawls's positioning of political Liberalism as the only alternative to patently undesirable forms of religious belief and un-democracy is highly suspect.

Consider the way in which this move is made, with regard to various more-or-less non-religious views or practices that are sure to strike Rawls's main/implied audience as self-evidently undesirable. Notice the way that Rawls positions Liberalism as the only obvious alternative to these, and these as the only obvious alternatives to Liberalism:

> The wars of [the twentieth] century with their extreme violence and increasing destructiveness, culminating in the manic evil of the Holocaust, raise in an acute way the question whether political relations must be governed by power and coercion alone. If a reasonably just society that subordinates power to its aims is not possible and people are largely amoral, if not incurably cynical and self-centered, one might ask with Kant whether it is worthwhile for human beings to live on the earth. We must start with the assumption that a reasonably just political society is possible ... [*A Theory of Justice*] and [*Political Liberalism*] try to sketch what the more reasonable conceptions of justice for a democratic regime are and to present a candidate for the most reasonable.[7]

No other options are considered, besides the most appalling tyranny on the one hand and liberal governance on the other. There is no question of people being self-organizing (as in anarchism – compare the mode of life described by George Orwell in *Homage to Catalonia* – and in some kibbutzim in the past, for instance), and/or living on the basis (say) of love rather than justice. Rawls's political rhetoric, presenting a stark choice between the justice of a liberal regime on the one hand and the road to the Holocaust and the Gulag and '9/11' on the other, is subtly politically manipulative. Once one has *picked* how Rawls's rhetoric functions, he starts to seem, on the one hand, good-hearted to the point of naivety (in his expectation of a clean moral politics in 'liberal democracies' supposedly based on justice, the rule of law and 'public reason,' not dominated by corporate greed or by the artificial creation of 'needs' through marketing); and, on the other hand, question-begging and self-contradictory (in the claim to 'neutrality'). 'Liberalism or barbarism' might very easily be Rawls's motto hereabouts. The possibility of a non-liberal non-barbarism is simply not raised.

Compare this passage: 'various religious sects oppose the culture of the modern world and wish to lead their common life apart from its foreign influences'.[8] Well; *I* for one oppose the 'culture of the modern world', insofar as it is individualistic, exploitative, craven in its kow-towing to commerce, philistinic, and so on. But once more, the kind of positively altered education system that someone like me would want to put in place to help engender a better culture does not get heard by Rawls: only the negative case of the extremists moves him. Rawls presumes that his readers will have a negative image of and instinctive reaction against 'sects' which 'oppose the culture of the modern world'. This latter, I suggest, is a very telling presumption.

Liberalism rules out having a state educational system which 'indoctrinates' children into a love for one another and for the planet, a treating of these as sacred, in the very same gesture as it rules out having a state educational system which indoctrinates them into Islam or evangelical Christianity. In doing so, I contend, it throws out the baby – it throws out our children – with the bathwater. What it rules in is an educational system hollowed out of the sacred and of meaning, fit only for raising children to be little consumers, 'choosing' freely what they consider to be good and nagging their parents til those items are bought for them ...

Liberalism can tolerate religions only if they either strip themselves of 'intrinsic' aspects (i.e. are no longer truly a way of life and are therefore in the end of no deep significance for their practitioners), or if their 'intrinsic' aspects are basically unthreatening to liberalism (if they preach simply 'withdrawal' from the public world – to the extent permitted by law!). If one believes that true religion, true spirituality, is necessarily *engaged*, then one will accept neither of these. Again, that goes just as much for many (I would claim) desperately needed and positive life-affirming religions and spiritualities – that Rawls says virtually nothing about – as it does for the religious fundamentalisms that Rawls scares his readers with by repeatedly invoking seemingly as the only alternative to his 'impartial' approach.

But what, some readers might complain, *is* the option I have left them? For there may seem to be a contradiction in my analysis of western Liberalism's relationship to religion if (as I hope) it is obvious that as I say what I have done above, I am at the same time an avid believer in most substantive civil liberties (liberties which our 'leading' western 'liberal' states are currently discarding with remarkable speed and near-alacrity, and which are being best defended, it seems to me, by the very radical direct-action groups which are at best barely tolerated in the 'liberal democratic' polity), in real freedom of expression and a well-informed citizenry (incompatible with a capitalist 'free' press), in a genuine democracy (rather than a merely formal freedom to vote), and in equality (rather than the *in*equality manifested in 'the difference principle'). It *must be*, such readers will (rightly) conclude, that I am somehow claiming that one does not have to endorse liberal principles of political philosophy in order to believe in these things. I have argued that it might, in fact, even be that there is little chance of these things being preserved or ever achieved unless we discard the un-self-aware fundamentalism that is liberalism and embrace instead a frankly non-'neutral', spiritually rich, green and localized vision for humankind,[9] a vision in which the siren call of religious fundamentalism can be resisted, not, except *in* true *extremis* through being intolerated, but through the explicit putting forth of a rival conception of the human good that might actually win the battle for the hearts and souls and minds of the peoples of the Earth, in the 'marketplace of ideas'. But I have not as yet given an *example* of what such a religion might be. This lack of examples is at least as bad as Rawls's multiplicity of bad examples, one might claim.

So onto an example of a religion, or rather, a way of living a religious-type life, that is seemingly compatible with Liberalism's tolerance-talk, or rather with its putative 'acceptance' of various other forms of religious(-type) living, but which wonderfully avoids the risk of dogmatizing such tolerance-talk to the point that it precludes such earnest, meaningful religious-type living altogether: Quakerism.

Quakers (members of the 'Religious Society of Friends') avoid the peril of dogmatism outlined in Wittgenstein's epigram to this chapter precisely because Quakers (also called 'Friends') have no creed. At least, I want to argue, that Quakerism, when properly understood, requires no – and in fact is most truly 'religious' when denying any – dogmatic articles of faith, scriptures, characteristics of God (as problematic as affirming any of these things will be for some practitioners of *any* religion), and so on. This makes Friends almost unique among bodies with close historical ties and affinities to Christianity, and also perhaps in one fell swoop takes them partly outside that tradition (such that they're both inside and outside it, as it were).

But if this is so, if there is no body of doctrine, adherence to which constitutes membership, what is it that binds Friends together? What is it, more than anything else, that makes Friends keep talking to and being with and doing what we call 'worshipping' with Friends? What makes Friends Friends?[10] (For those readers familiar with Quakerism, I believe a hint is given by my rhetorical insistence upon the moniker 'Friends' – a term particularly apt at describing Quaker practice and equally rich in its secular resonances.)

Again, compared at least to most branches of Christianity, Quakerism is unique in its emphasis on practice, not necessarily in the sense of 'good works' but in the sense, compressedly speaking, of an active engagement by all in worship and in life outside formal worship. 'But how can this be? Surely what is and has always been important to Friends, as for "practitioners" of any religion, is faith AND practice?'

I have at this point to venture an uncomfortable hypothesis, one which I think must in its essentials be correct: that a traditional emphasis on faith and practice in the understanding of Quakerism specifically, but to some extent of religion *in general*, has to be recast such that faith in any supernaturalistic sense is only of significance if it is constitutive of *Quakerliness* (and, again, that part of most religions with which 'practitioners' actually *identify*)[11] insofar as it is essential to Quaker (or, if reading the comparison here, any religious) practice. How far is that? Not very far at all; for right away we have to ask, faith in what exactly? Not all Quakers would claim faith in God any more; or, at least, they would disagree profoundly about what God is. And who among Friends can justify (and how?) a *proprietary* claim on the terms 'religious' or 'God'?

If one believes that the projection of this Quaker tendency onto religions in general is tenuous at this point, I think a well-store of edifying examples of actually lived religious ceremonies (at least in the West) come to mind: of how many Catholics (particularly those who embrace the sort of baseline scientism that underlies their everyday lives) reciting the Nicene Creed, for example, could it appropriately be said that they actually *believe* that there will ever be an end of time, let alone one when the corpses of all dead Catholics will rise from the grave and be restored to the state of their lived-world prime? How many, for that matter, could be said to even *know or care* that this is the literal meaning of what they say when they affirm belief in 'the resurrection of the dead' during mass? The point is, literal meanings are not necessarily (really, hardly ever) the endgame in religious talk, or religious ceremonies; rather, they play a different role, and not purely a 'psychological' one.

I would venture that many people who can only be described as 'religious', and most especially some Quakers, would not even claim to have faith in anything aside from vagaries such as 'the Light in each and every one of us'. Such phrases as that, useful as they are, can hardly bind groups together very tightly.

To put this another way, couldn't the word 'faithfulness' in many instances be substituted for 'faith'? Possibly: faithfulness as an embodied attitude that need not directly imply faith in any one thing. But then faithfulness itself is a kind of practice.

Why is it that I feel it necessary to venture this unconventional 'practicist' hypothesis? Well, what is religion – again, especially 'in practice' – if not a kind of *seeking*; must we all be seeking exactly the same thing?

*   *   *

As described above, Quakerism provides an interesting playing out of how creedlessness, in tandem with tolerance for diverse spiritual practices – so long as these are not directly subversive of other Quaker practices, or of other Friends – can only imply that faith in the conventional sense *is simply not* an essential part of what it is to be who Quakers are collectively.

Haven't I just, though, with the above proviso 'so long as these are not directly subversive of other Quaker practices, or of other Friends', ceded the point to Rawlsian Liberalism? How is this different from political Liberalism's 'tolerance', as Rawls and others like to call it, of any ... tolerable religion? In other words, doesn't the proviso I've issued in reference to Quaker 'tolerance' really just try to sneak in precisely this Liberal proviso, the one on which I have based a number of significant attacks on Liberalism above?

What, in greater specificity, constitutes 'Quaker practice' and what makes *this* so markedly different from (many, most?)[12] other religious practices so as to keep the limited tolerance of Quakers from collapsing into the artificial 'tolerance' of political Liberalism?

Well, many things; but, very centrally, Quaker practice is what Friends do in Meeting, namely they go to Meeting (silent Meeting for Worship),[13] they *constitute* Meeting. And they *demand* nothing more or less of each other than a sincere and non-hostile effort at so constituting Meeting, at being Friends. They once did demand more than this, and they may still ask and want (for) more; but this is all that they *demand* of each other, *in virtue* of being Quakers (as opposed to in virtue of being close – ordinary, small-'f' – friends, or members of a worship-sharing group).

How does this mark a sort of tolerance (or the requirements of practice) different from that of most religions; that is to say, (how) *does* this really make Quakers somehow more or differently tolerant than practitioners of most other religions?

I have contended that there are no principles any more that are central to Quakerism save for principles of practice. That is, the practice of sitting and waiting in silence, inside Meeting and life, with the discipline and 'spirit' of these practices, of almost continually working one's self mentally and spiritually along with others. But this may or may not involve any supernaturalistic faith; all it *necessarily* involves is a rather particular kind of action. When one looks at many other religions, one generally sees this less often. One often sees, instead, gold and ornamentation, physical places (as opposed to actions or people) set aside as 'sacred' and marked or cordoned off in various ways, and trappings held as necessary to mediate between people and religious 'experiences'.

But in fact we should grant that there are anti-essentialist, non-creedal practitioners of each religion. There are some in each religion who would hold that it is the people *gathering* (*doing* and *being* together) that constitute the religion and not, for example, the adherence to anything metaphysical, etc. There is a 'contemplative' branch to Islam, for instance: Sufism. The difference with Quakerism – and with some eastern traditions such as Buddhism – is that the meditative and action-rather-than-supernaturalistic-faith-based side of the religion *is* dominant. Intriguingly, many meditative and contemplative religious people tend to be genuinely tolerant of other religions.

To argue that deeply felt religious tolerance can be the same across deeply felt religious boundaries is to hold that, in general, deeply felt religion is incommensurate with the subordinating of itself to the state *prioritat* that political Liberalism claims is necessary for defending the neutrality of that state and its citizens. For when religious people are liberal or tolerant *as a matter of their religion*, then it is the state, the political-social Liberal infrastructure of laws, that is rendered irrelevant. To put this another way, Rawls might sit out- (or in-) side of a Friends Meeting and say to himself, 'They are tolerant, and law-abiding; what good political Liberalists these fellows are' while all of the Friends at the meeting may be ignorant of [*A Theory of Justice*], [*Political Liberalism*], Rawls himself, the 'theory' of Liberalism in general, and so on. The Friends inside might even be (as I am) *opposed* to such a theory; they might, for instance, believe as Quakers that peace is a cause that overrides the state's laws and claims upon them.

*   *   *

There are some analogies between the way that practice is paramount for 'contemplative' (as opposed to creedal) religions such as Quakerism, on the one hand, and Thomas Kuhn's well-known (if much-misunderstood) notion of 'new paradigms' and 'paradigm-shift', on the other.[14] When scientists start to notice the need for a new 'paradigm' (or overarching theory), because of problems with the consistency or empirical adequacy of an existing theory or theories, they suddenly find that they have all sorts of disagreements about what they believe *now*, about what the existing theory *is* exactly. These differences in belief never needed to come out before, because all the members of the community of scientists did the same thing, because they shared a certain scientific practice – they did the same kinds of experiments – which was (and will be again, once a new theoretical paradigm is settled upon and eventually fades into the background) the important thing for the community of scientists in question. Similarly, that is what is important for Quakers, I claim. The difference in our case is that religions, unlike sciences (so long, that is, as they do not try supernaturalistically to ape the sciences), are never *forced* to change paradigms, never *forced* to agree explicitly upon a new set of beliefs, because religions thankfully have utterly different standards of 'consistency' and 'empirical adequacy'; indeed, the latter is largely irrelevant. Thus Quakers and other relevant religious groups relevantly similar to them need never reach the point of 'duking it out' over ideology and theology, because they share a central common emphasis on practice as *the* important thing.

There is, I think, at least one religion that cannot be so defended: political Liberalism itself! Indeed, in its insistence on its own priority, political Liberalism is a 'secular' *fundamentalism*. Its pseudo-non-religious character masks its absolutely imperial reach, its *comprehensive* (re-)conception of the totality of human life (compare the epigraph above). Liberalism's claim to neutrality, which has made liberal political philosophy appear as if it is the only game in town in the contemporary English-speaking academic world, is an ideological charade, masking its now-fully-global ambition for spiritual and political dominance.[15] I therefore reject, possibly as a matter of religious conviction, liberalism as deeply dangerous as well as self-contradictory.

To conclude, then: religion without belief, without faith (in the usual, dogmatic sense of these words), can be a damn good thing! Liberalism neuters religion by restricting it to being nothing *but* belief. But religion that matters is *practice*. And such practice is, often, necessarily 'political'. Don't forget that Quakers led the struggle against slavery and Quakers have refused to go to war. Quakers' 'peace testimony', their *conscientious objection*, their increasing interest in freeing animals from human domination, is unacceptable to Liberalism. So much the better for Quakers (and Mennonites, and the Seventh Day Adventists, among Christians), and so much the worse for Liberalism.

Positive, life-affirming religions and spiritualities such as Quakerism will, I believe, overcome Liberalism while preserving and affirming religious tolerance in the twenty-first century. This, at least, is a cause for optimism. Engaged spirituality and religion may yet stop the juggernaut of war and of ecological disaster that Liberal political philosophy has tended, tragically, to underwrite, in states such as the USA and the UK. Religion 'without belief' may well be religion which has vital, good, spiritual and political consequences, within our lifetimes.

4 Which is Worse: Death or Dying?

This is not an essay on voluntary euthanasia. For the record, it is for this writer obvious that people who are quite set on the course of ending their own lives, particularly when they are in great pain and highly unlikely to be relieved of that pain in the near future, must be permitted to do so.

My topic, while perhaps related and an issue every bit as personal as the right to die at the right time, differs from it in being applicable to every one of us, not just to those few (even if – because of new technologies or other improvements in medicine, hospice care, and so on – their numbers increase every year) who are forced by circumstances unexpectedly to choose between a little bit more of a very painful life or a hastened death. The issue I will focus on here is perhaps the one question that never dies, one of the few that has seemingly been with us since before Socrates chose the hemlock and Jesus the cross: which is worse, *death or dying*?

But prior to answering this, there are two preliminary questions that we must attend to: what is it that we fear about death? and what is it that we fear about dying? I will address these questions purely from the 'first person' point of view, because the loss of a loved one as experienced by others not only requires separate treatment but is, I think, largely separable, in that the questions prompted are merely *related* to, rather than partially *constituent* of, the question of one's *own* death or dying.

About our own death we fear: firstly, our own extinguishment; secondly, what comes after death.

About our dying, we fear: firstly, the visceral *anticipation* of our own extinguishment; secondly, the pain and suffering usually involved in the actual process of being extinguished ('dying').

Comparing these two: on the first count, there is not any very great difference, for we know we are mortal and in a sense must always be prepared for death and dying (there is no question of our avoiding either fate, or either fear). Insofar as there is a difference, it must point pretty *definitively* towards dying being worse than death – for one's *actual* extinguishment is not something one experiences;[1] while in the course of dying, one is highly likely to experience vividly the awareness of this impending non-existence. On the second count, dying is pretty *clearly* worse than death, for – as those of us who are not self-deluded are aware (but see below) – nothing comes after death. There is only extinguishment. While something – viz. more or less excruciating agony – usually does *precede* death.

Taking these two counts together, then, it appears quite clear that dying must be worse than death. And I believe that this is correct, for there is nothing to fear about death itself – about nothingness – except for the peculiar fact of our being nothing when dead. While dying is tied almost inexorably to myriad terrors.

But a nagging worry about this argument remains: it doesn't always *seem* or *feel* as *obvious* as this that death is in essence comparatively unfearing, does it? Can the eternal question of death and dying really be *as easy to answer* as I have thus far suggested? And what might our nagging feeling that something has been missed signify?

Perhaps this: that even the process of being extinguished – even living in continual abject terror or torment – may be a more welcome prospect when compared to nothingness. Or rather, that it may at least seem this way to us when we are forced by unexpected circumstances to attempt to contemplate – *really* contemplate – our own future non-existence [see p. 62 below].

(Some have suspected that we simply cannot do this, that we are constitutively unable to grasp the concept of our own impending non-existence. If there is something to this thought – which we cannot investigate in detail here – *the reason why* may be brought out by the circular *'impasse'* brought out below.)

All this brings us back to the fear of what comes after death. Might this, too, be a substitute for, a displacement of, the fear of the unthinkable, of the after-death, of one's own *non-existence*? Here would be an explanation of precisely how a vastly influential religious delusion might 'deviously' serve a positive psychic purpose – 'surviving on' after physical extinguishment – even when it *appears* at its least attractive and hardest to swallow, that is when it *appears* to constitute a motive people might have for *not* believing and for having an easy time of it 'in this life' instead – that is, 'surviving on' in a hell, an eternal torment.

Now, for those of us who believe we have – or, better, simply *have* – experienced hell on Earth, this is a fascinating and somewhat disarming idea. I myself have at least once attempted to size up the degree of the ongoing horror I was facing and chose death instead, only then to be seared still deeper by the paralysing thought that perhaps death as the end of lived experience – death as I (had) conceived it – was *not an option*; that there might *only* be indefinitely prolonged horror and terror. (In a fuller presentation one might with profit analyse whether it makes any difference in a purely *psychological* sense to conceive of indefinitely prolonged terror on Earth as opposed to 'in the after-life'.) It may have been only a latent awareness of how far I was from actually taking decisive steps to kill myself that prompted this searing, scorching realization; but I suspect that it was rather the sheer vertigo of this paralysing thought, a thought I would have given virtually anything to have un-thought and thus a thought which it would be *so* good to be able to disarm. How good it can be, against this backdrop, only to have to face the concept of nothingness, not of everlastingness.

Sadly, however, the 'explanation' of the delusion of immortality I have given above can also start in its turn to seem an overly tempting and perhaps self-delusive thought in such a context. That is, 'Maybe everlasting torment, the absolute misery of the eternal moment of hell *isn't* so *bad* after all' risks of course being just one more vain quasi-therapeutic hope to abate the terror of unending terror. And one is even forced back to asking oneself once more: is it perhaps we would-be sanguine non-theists who are self-deludedly running away from the awful, nagging possibility that, after all, death is as nothing (as it were ...) compared to the agony of non-death in a terrible, tedious, everlasting hell on Earth as in 'the after-life'? That is, is there any perspective from which to view the opposing possibilities of anything other than a heavenly existence-after-death (because 'surviving on' in some sort of eternal bliss is a completely other sort of possible delusion) that makes it clear who such a thought it benefiting?

Confused? I certainly am. It seems just impossible to tell, now, what one is trying hardest to avoid: the *unimaginable* awfulness of going from all this wonder to sheer non-existence, on the one hand, or the *extreme* awfulness of 'hell', or (similarly) the (all-too-imaginable?) awfulness of (a painful) dying, on the other?

We seem by this point to have become locked into a circular dialectic that itself threatens to be indefinitely prolonged (as we shall see in considering some attempts to end it or even to evade it): a dialectic of thought about these most harrowing of personal thoughts in action. There is *no way* to decide with finality which is worse – non-existence or continual torment – not because we haven't (of course!) experienced them, but simply because, whichever one decides for, one will inevitably appear to be trying to escape from the full horror of facing up to the other. And *here*, appearance *is* reality; for both of these 'options' are, from a first-person perspective, likely to seem nothing other than infinitely awful – unmitigated – disasters.

What I am suggesting is that it may be impossible to think about and feel and face questions of one's own death or dying in good faith. (One might say, nothingness and indefinitely prolonged agony are 'incommensurable': one cannot *measure* them against each other.) This is arguably a difficulty common to several issues that are heavily constitutive of ourselves and in which the stakes are very high (another less harrowing example would be one's attitude towards one's immediate relatives; in particular, whether one was glad to have the nuclear family one has, or not to have had siblings, etc.). Issues such as this are so pressing and overpowering, and one's pre-existing, more-or-less inchoate ideas concerning them are so integral a part of who and what one is, that bad faith concerning them is just unavoidable, however clearly or deeply one thinks.

'Doesn't all this speculation rest on an untenable or undesirable individualistic egoism?' No, only facing squarely the facticity of one's own mortality. The lunatic or the ineffably calm nature-lover or the saint who can face *quite entirely without regret* the prospect of her body's decline and return to the soil is, in my view, para-human and simply not the kind of person with whom I can hope authentically to communicate (here or elsewhere). Not even the great traditions of Buddhism – which, if anything could, would offer a solution to the problem under discussion in this essay – can claim seriously to *eliminate* the regret at death or the boggle at non-existence that I have been discussing. That, after all, is why Buddhism has so often hyperbolically reached for ideas of Buddahood entirely transcending humanity, or has fallen back into fantasies of reincarnation or of actually-existing hells. (A true Buddhism, in my opinion and experience, is about *reconciling* oneself to one's fears and delusions and desires, such that their power over one diminishes, and not about *extinguishing* or *eliminating* them.)

'But again, isn't the "option" of continual torment a false one, because the notion of immortality is the biggest delusion of them all, and nothing short of immortality could eventuate in *continual* torment?' The last clause here is precisely what must be put into question – though it is admittedly probably only the experience of a timeless instant of unredeemed horror that could persuade someone of this. Those of us who have experienced such moments understand all too well the mystics who mutter that 'to live in the present moment is to live in – to experience – eternity'. A key mistake of traditional theology has been precisely its insistence that eternity – whether of bliss or of suffering – is *necessarily* not of this Earth, that it requires a literal infinity of moments, an infinite/immortal existence.

'Is the "option" of non-existence itself really so terrible? For nothing has been said here about why it should be so; after all, once one became non-existent, one would of course feel no terror'. Indeed, as made clear above, it is in a sense our anticipation of death that is terrible, not death in itself, which, as Wittgenstein wrote, is (unlike dying) 'not an event in life'.[2] But that this is so is in a sense trivial: it is – of course – I (the writer) and you (the reader), who, non-dead, are in dialogue and *contemplating* non-existence. It is such contemplation and its effects in practice that constitute our being, in Heidegger's words, a 'being-toward-death'.[3] And, once again, if one has not experienced the infinite sadness, the sometimes endless vertiginous desolation of conceiving of one's own utter disappearance, of the snuffing out of one's experiences and actions, then it cannot be explained to one. (Though it helps if you self-consciously give up the chimera of achieving immortality through your offspring. And great art may help too; compare the closing scenes of *Blade Runner*, in which two quasi-human 'replicants' (and their Blade Runner go-between) are forced to contemplate their own extraordinarily precise mortality (they are allotted an exact – short – lifespan by their human creators).)[4]

A final objection: 'Is this whole treatment not vitiated by the cold, over-intellectualized manner in which it has been pursued? Doesn't this abstraction miss something that is, to borrow a word first used when assaying what is to be feared in dying, *visceral* about the consideration of death and dying?' To this I might make two responses. The first is that I have tried to say something intelligible about a highly complex, befuddling and seductive question; and that this may be the only way I can *write* about it at all. The alternative is simply to scream. The other response is that the consequence of such deliberations can be, at best, only *part* of the treatment of the philosophical problem, and that what remains cannot be thought, but must instead be lived.

In other words, there is room to think that living in a certain way can help one approach the bad faith arguably unavoidable in the consideration of one's own death and dying *in good faith* – that is, to honestly address the host of emotions, confusions and (possibly) actions accompanying our stupor in the face of that problem, to try, *in* one's life, to establish a *legacy*, conscious of the tempting but nonsensical prospect that doing so might constitute some kind of immortality. To rephrase the Heideggerian 'being-toward-death', to render ourselves – through living in such a way as to impact some condition of the world that will persist after our death like fighting cataclysmic global climate change, for a more even distribution of international wealth, to influence the machinery of the state in which you (and others, to be sure) live, etc. (in short, living politically and ethically while alive)[5] – 'beings-toward(-the)-life(-of-others)'. What's more, this sort of living can be done even while we are conscious of our impending extinguishment (and as such should not be confused with the sort of carefree indifference about death that many associate with adolescence, nihilism, or (wrongly) existentialism). This (book) is philosophy for life, after all.

In tandem with the so-called 'over-intellectualized' examination carried out in the greater three-quarters of this essay, this 'being-toward-life' also serves to deflate much of the

existential angst about nothingness against which indefinitely
prolonged torment can be seen as a desirable eventuality
(see p. 57 above), and it makes a further contribution to the
discussion of the fear of what comes after death. Recall my
claim that such thought, prompted out of a devotion to some
(usually) religiously based life-after-death scenario, could 'serve
a positive psychic purpose even when it appears at its least
attractive and hardest to swallow'. Is this positive psychic effect
caused by either 1). simply the notion that our consciousness
(our 'being') will persist after death, whether in suffering or
bliss,[6] or 2). the more complex notion of an ethereal *reward*
for life lived a certain way on Earth? As is clear, both options
necessitate the persistence of consciousness, which (as discussed
above) is the very possibility which gives rise to the threat
that perpetual torment might, on second thought, be worse
than everlastingness. (This is, of course, the 'circular impasse'
referred to above.) By contrast, a political or social commitment
– say, to altering the terms by which a society will discuss,
after your death, something like the existence of non-human
animals, or people of differing races or creeds – leaving an
impact on the world after death allows for some persistence,
just not of consciousness. And while, certainly, this possibility
does not assuage many of the terrors rising out of the threat
of non-existence – for in large part it is just the non-existence
itself which is terrifying, as opposed to the thought that,
without existence, we can *do* nothing to affect the perception of
ourselves by others – it certainly does help both to mollify some
of the visceral panic about the status and value of our existences
(especially when that panic is raised by the realization of a life
less than perfectly lived) and (consequently) to make the 'cold-
intellectualizing' of the problem itself less artificial.

In sum: if you actually live, and live in a way that is not
self-obsessed, you will not be so scared of death *or* dying.

The riddle of death – and dying – will surely continue to be
central to our being no matter how it twists and swerves with

the times, and with new technologies. What I have given here is a reason for believing that it is a riddle without a solution. The most we can hope for – though perhaps it would be quite enough – is for our lives to turn us away from the dialectical paradox that results from it and towards a *dissolution* of its power over us. This power for psychic harm – also, *perhaps*, for enlightenment – may thus become less central, *less*. And one may then live, *more*, by living for others, including others who will come afterwards, along the lines that I have just indicated.

There is no *road* back from anticipation of one's own dissolution. Sadly and ironically, not even a piece of writing such as this, (even) if it is on target, can possibly hope to be even a signpost down such a road, just because it (this chapter) implies that there is no such road, no solution to the riddle, and because the kind of thinking it requires and encourages is itself caught up in the riddle, in the *impasse*. The dissolution of the riddle of one's own dissolution cannot be *accomplished* by oneself, or by others. It can only *non-reflectively*, gradually, possibly, *happen*, possibly *influenced* by how one chooses to live. Possibly; before one dies.[7]

5 (How) Is Forgiveness Possible?

In order to get a grip on this extreme and seemingly very general question, it will be handy for us to have a good example or two of situations where forgiveness clearly seems called for:

[A] Imagine that you are reading this book along with somebody else. As you go to turn the page, they rather clumsily knock their coffee over, spilling it all over you and over the printed page. Imagine something like the following dialogue ensuing:

> They: 'Oh I'm terribly sorry; that was clumsy and stupid of me. Here, let me help clean you up; sorry!'
> You: 'Don't worry, y'know don't worry, it's not that important; I know you didn't "mean it".'
> They: 'No no, really – it really was very stupid; oh dear ... do please forgive me.'

Now, if they in their agitation and regret really did say this, what would you say then? What would be your response to this request for absolution? In the case of such a trivial event, it's quite likely that you would soon enough say something like the following:

> You: 'Don't worry, don't be silly, there's nothing to forgive, really; it's nothing.'

Let's ponder that phrase for a moment. 'There's nothing to forgive'. Let's for the sake of argument assume that you actually meant what you said (and were not, for example, merely being polite, while deep down you seethed and said to yourself, 'That was simply *unforgivably* clumsy!'). If so, it will be important and unavoidable to pay attention to the way that this piece of language actually works. If we can, *prima facie*, we should try to save the appearances of any piece of language.[1] We should try to take seriously the use of locutions such as 'There's nothing to forgive', if we can. Perhaps we can't. It's only the exception, not the rule, I would suggest, that we – and our words – don't mean what we (they) say.

So; if we take the sentence, 'There's nothing to forgive' seriously, if then there really is nothing to forgive in the example we have sketched, then quite clearly we haven't as yet got before us an example where forgiveness is relevant.

* * *

Let's try another example.

[B] Imagine that the person sitting beside you, while the two of you were silently reading, simply picked up the cup of coffee and quite deliberately *threw* it all over you.

* * *

Or

[C] Think – actually think right now – of an example, a real instance, where you have been deliberately or at least knowingly treated badly/maliciously, in the past. Think of a betrayal or a serious deception practised on you by someone you trusted.

* * *

If we're thinking of an action like B or C, then the question perhaps is not, is forgiveness necessary at all here? but rather, *how can forgiveness happen at all here*?

Some wrong actions can in a way be undone. For instance, if I accidentally spill coffee over your beloved book, maybe I can buy you another one, just the same as the first. But actions that stand in need of forgiveness are often not like this. Something is broken that cannot *simply* be replaced/repaired. If there is to be repair in the relationship, something more is required: say, repentance and forgiveness. But again, how to forgive, even the repentant, in a case like B or C above? How to forgive, when forgiveness is required? When a breach has been effected, when something undoable has been done?

Now, it would seem reasonable to suppose that it would be *straightforward* to answer that question if forgiveness were of the following nature: *if the past actually changed, when forgiveness was sought and granted*. If by being asked for forgiveness, and then granting that forgiveness, the past could be altered, the deed undone. Then, I take it, it would be clear why in many cases forgiveness was desirable, why it was engaged in – and why it was/is wonderful. But this scenario is of course utter fantasy. What actually happens is: a harm or wrong is done, it remains a wrong and yet it gets … forgiven. This is the extraordinary thing, the thing that somehow we have to hang on to: that a wrong that remains a wrong, that is not undone, somehow gets transformed in its felt meaning. It is no longer felt bitterly and/or acted upon accordingly.

When we think of an action such as B or C above, and we think of its being forgiven, the whole thing can come to seem more and more bizarre or remarkable. What is this thing called … forgiveness? What can it mean, for something like – something called – 'forgiving' to happen?

*   *   *

Now, typically, when philosophers start asking themselves a question like that, they start by trying to think of some set of concepts or categories which they might effectively use to explicate, analyse, or at least analogize the troublesome concept in question. So; I'm starting to have some real trouble getting a grip on what forgiveness is, on what 'forgiveness' could possibly be said intelligibly to mean – on how forgiveness is possible. What forgiveness is, how forgiveness is possible at all … I'm starting to have trouble with that, so I'll try looking to other concepts which I have less trouble with.

(I) Ceasing to punish *X*/ceasing to demand that *X* repay a debt

Etymology fans tend to like this rendition of forgiveness. And more importantly: we know what it means to do one of these things. So these formulations *could* help us.

But a moment's reflection makes it evident that these concepts are not going to give us nearly enough resources with which to understand forgiveness. One can decide to forgive a debt, for example, because, hey, it's only money; or just because it will be really difficult in practical terms to get the money back. But in the latter case, for instance, one may well nevertheless feel considerable bitterness towards the debtor.

There are all sorts of practical reasons why one might cease to demand the repayment of a debt, or cease to punish – but what forgiveness is, for us, is clearly more than (I). The harm was done. That in itself can't be undone; forgiveness is more than (I).

Unless we are to understand the sense of 'punish' or 'debt' here in a 'full' or 'deep' sense. Unless, for example, we mean by ceasing to punish something like 'ceasing to harbour resentment'. But in that case, we have merely re-described the problem. For this is what we want to understand: how can it be possible to cease to harbour resentment for a wrong that can't be undone?

* * *

(II) Understanding

A second candidate: is *understanding* sufficient for forgiveness?
Is it the case that when one comes to *understand* why x
did y, then that can be tantamount to or at least directly
and immediately conducive to forgiveness? If so, then we
might be in good shape, because surely we understand what
'understanding' is, right?

I shall come back to this question below. But first, to tackle
the question of whether really understanding why x did y can
directly yield forgiveness. Because I'm not at all sure that it
can.

A slogan perhaps comes to mind: 'To understand all is to
forgive all'. But is that claim actually true? For sure, sometimes
one finds that upon closer investigation, having made an effort
to understand the 'forgivee', one changes one's view of the
incident in question substantively – one comes to identify with
the 'wrongdoer' to such an extent that one no longer thinks
that any wrong was done, but thinks that, on the contrary, they
acted rightly or at least in some justifiable way. And, for sure,
sometimes one finds that, in the case of an apparent betrayal
or deception, the whole thing rested on … a misunderstanding.
There was an equivocation on a word, or a word was
misheard or misattributed, for example. The 'betrayal' was
merely accidental; in other words, non-existent. So, for sure,
sometimes – in both the above kinds of cases – understanding
why someone did something results in its turning out that
there's nothing to forgive. But then we are back to case A,
above. And so we do not have here any cases where forgiveness
is in question. 'To understand all', in these cases, is actually to
see that no forgiveness is required.

If we turn to cases which *are* within our purview, where
forgiveness *is* 'required', then it is much less obvious that
'understanding all' will solve the problem. Sometimes one
hopes, perhaps desperately, that talking with the person who

wronged one will enable one to see their action in quite a new light, but (sometimes) what actually emerges is that they were doing the whole thing *more* maliciously than one had at first thought, e.g.: 'What, you mean actually that this ... this *affair* has been going on for *years*, and you've systematically deceived and betrayed me over this person, even knowing that I was practically bound to find out in the end?!'

It seems quite evident that there are at least some cases – important cases – where understanding is not equal to forgiving, but where in fact *the contrary* is most likely to be true. And it seems evident also that, as we saw above, where understanding does apparently lead to forgiveness, what actually happens is that the action is removed from the set of actions that produce a need for forgiveness. Presumably, the following is going to be an unsatisfactory philosophical analysis of forgiveness: that the acts one 'forgives' someone for turn out to be acts that precisely do not require or produce a need for forgiveness!

And, after all, none of this should really much surprise us. Because the idea that to understand all is to forgive all is not really an idea that suggests only a laudable tolerance and empathy, but rather a dubious relativism. There are at least some cases where, even if understanding can be achieved, it is not evident that forgiveness should or could be granted.[2] (And, concomitantly, if there is real forgiveness, it cannot be that the wrong done is in any way changed or lessened – indeed, that would often be a failure, a moral failure, a suspect weakening of moral judgement. Whereas my sense is that a remarkable feature of true forgiveness is that it involves a kind of moral *strengthening*.)

So it seems to me that, for the reasons just given, the concept of understanding offers us very little help at all in the project of understanding *forgiveness*. For where it most powerfully can appear to offer such help, it only does so by removing actions from the category of 'wrong'. What we want to understand, to say it once again, is actions which are wrong, but – somehow – forgiven.

It might be objected at this point that I have not considered enough different varieties of 'understanding'; and that a variety exists according to which the slogan 'To understand all is to forgive all' could be saved. (This returns us to a question with which we began this section – 'have we to hand an adequate understanding of "understanding"?') '"Understanding" is a family resemblance concept', it might be urged, and I fully agree. 'You don't understand what the advocate of (II) is saying', it might be urged; 'They are saying that if you *really* understand – fully and deeply – then you will forgive, or will have forgiven'. Once again, such a proposal can hardly be objected to – except to say that once again it merely reproduces our problem. There are indeed some uses of the term 'understand' (e.g. in some religious contexts, *vis-à-vis* 'religious experience') in which the use of the word 'understanding' has the character which the objector here urges. But to understand what it is – and how it is possible – to understand in this 'full' way is exactly what we need to … understand. In such a use, we do not yet, I think, adequately understand what 'understanding' is. To do so is precisely our task in this chapter. Let us then try another candidate:

(III) Forgetting

Is 'forgetting' the key to forgiving? Perhaps another slogan, a popular invocation or instruction, comes to mind, 'Forgive and forget'.

Right away we notice that the slogan 'Forgive *and* forget' suggests a differentiation. And while I think that there is an important connection between forgiving and forgetting – indeed, that forgetting is in some cases *criterial* for forgiving – it is relatively easy to show that understanding 'forgetting' will not enable us to understand forgiving, that there remains a gulf between them. A cute philosopher's counter-example should be enough to make clear that not just any mode of forgetting will amount to forgiveness:

Imagine case [C] again. Soon after the betrayal or whatever, imagine that you suffer an accident – a serious head injury. You wake up in hospital. Your friend/lover/whoever comes to visit. You act very nicely towards them. They may well think that you have forgiven them, and are quite ready to be reconciled with them, to accept them back into your life and so forth – but actually, unfortunately, it's just that you've suffered a head injury. You've forgotten all about their heinous act …

Forgetting is obviously not sufficient for forgiveness; but it does offer a clue: there is a serious question about whether forgiveness can survive continual reminiscence. If one continually, or obsessively, remembers, then one surely hasn't forgiven. What we want out of 'forgiveness' is for something not to be continually present to one, but for one to be able to look at the person who has done the wrongful act, recognize that it was them who carried it out, and yet somehow overcome resentment.

'Forgetting' offers a clue – but no more than that.

One more try, a concept which has already crept into the margins of the paper, and may appear to offer our best and last hope:

(IV) Acceptance

Straightaway, we must subdivide 'acceptance' into at least two different kinds, and consider these more or less separately:

Accepting that *something has happened*

Is forgiveness that? Again, this concept seems to me to offer a clue – but to remain less than forgiveness. One can come to accept that a wrong act took place, and not feel that it is literally unbelievable that this horrible thing should have happened – one can, as it were, reconcile *with oneself* that one was betrayed – and yet resentment against the other may not be overcome.

Accepting an apology

A second variety of acceptance, and the one which will most intensively require our attention: is forgiveness relevantly analogous to accepting an apology? It would be great if it were, for accepting an apology is, roughly, 'a speech act'. That is: an utterance that *accomplishes* a non-verbal task when uttered. (Compare taking wedding vows: when a celebrant says 'I now pronounce you ...', several important, and not purely psychological, things happen – one's legal obligations change, etc.) And after what I hinted at earlier by referring to preserving the meaning of the verbal string – 'there's nothing to forgive' – many will agree that we, typically, understand speech acts.

If forgiveness can be understood by analogy to or on the model of a speech act, such as accepting an apology, then it seems that we will be able to understand it after all. And starting with 'accepting an apology' seems particularly promising, because it suggests the element of 'contrition' and dialogic reciprocity which seems likely to be crucial to any wise forgiving.

But regrettably ... no. Forgiveness cannot be as well understood as a speech act. Accepting an apology: sure, that can be pretty much understood in the same way that promising can be understood. When I accept an apology, I understand that you are regretful, and sincere in that regret, and I show this. But I may yet regret having to accept the apology, or find it hard to do so. I may, literally or metaphorically, accept an apology through gritted teeth.

But there cannot, I submit, be any such thing as forgiving through gritted teeth. Uttering the words 'I forgive you' with an ugly scowl playing around one's face – or simply in one's mind – is *not* forgiving someone. Roughly: if one says 'I forgive you' through gritted teeth, one is lying, or at best deceiving oneself.

So, forgiveness is clearly more than acceptance of an apology.

But what if someone were to respond to me at this point by saying, 'Maybe; but nevertheless "I forgive you" is itself a form of words, and its utterance must have some felicity conditions; why should we not understand forgiveness just through adequately understanding the speech act of saying "I forgive you"?'

But: a direct speech-act-analysis of 'I forgive you' is not – for reasons already indicated – going to work either. We *can*, for sure, have a fairly effective speech-act-analysis/understanding of 'accepting an apology' or, to return to the *locus classicus*, of 'promising'. If I say to you, 'I promise you that I'll go to the cinema with you next weekend', and then I don't go … well, in that case I have broken my promise. There are only some very specific circumstances in which a promise can be shown to be null and void, to have been infelicitously made or otherwise rendered invalid. But in the case of forgiveness, things are very different. You may have said to your betrayer, 'I forgive you for *y*', and a week passes, or a year passes … and it can *turn out* that you haven't in fact forgiven them. It can turn out, when one, as it were, looks within oneself, later, or if one, *or if others*, look at one's actual actions towards the wrongdoer since the declaration of forgiveness … it can turn out that one hasn't in fact forgiven them.

If someone breaks a promise, you can say to them, 'You broke your promise!' and there it makes no sense for the other to reply 'It "turns out" that I didn't promise you anything!' But I think that there are indefinitely many circumstances in which it can *turn out* that one hasn't forgiven another after all. Circumstances, cases in which it can turn out that re-occurrences of resentment – in mind or action – show this, perhaps much to one's – sometimes to everyone's – regret. Such re-occurrences can at virtually any time defeat the *attempt* one has made to forgive. This is how forgivers – all of us, potentially, not just an unsuccessful or 'hysterical' minority – suffer from reminiscences.

It seems, then, that, regrettably, the speech-act-analysis of forgiveness is by no means sufficient and that the additional component needed to yield a potentially adequate account of forgiveness is perhaps twofold. On the one hand, we might want to talk about ACCEPTING SOMEONE BACK INTO ONE'S LIFE, about certain kinds of behavioural changes. (But it is dangerous to say that this is *in general* necessary for forgiveness. There may be circumstances in which we might wish to allow for the possibility of forgiveness – so a physically or psychologically abused child might forgive – but not want to insist that the forgiver literally accept the forgivee back into her life, on pain of the forgiveness being otherwise described as fake. It is a common circumstance that one severely wronged will not forgive and so will not accept the wrongdoer back into their life; but I believe that there are cases where forgiveness too can accompany non-acceptance, in the sense currently under discussion.) Now: can one accept someone back into one's life *without* having forgiven them? Surely yes, for various imaginable practical purposes. Perhaps not, if the acceptance is deep and full and true … in which case we are just, familiarly now, repeating the mystery and the explanandum.

Rather than focusing upon changes in action, we might want to talk about – to give up-front priority to – a DEEP 'INNER' ACCEPTANCE, to talk about certain crucial kinds of emotional and mental changes, about a *change of heart*, a change of heart that takes place over time. Maybe such talk is, after all, the best we can do.

*   *   *

Is that the best we can do? We might talk about how such a 'change of heart' is very often tied to a changed attitude on the part of the wrongdoer. Is this as good as it gets? Is it good enough? Are we really any closer to understanding forgiveness – what it is, how it is possible – than we were at the start? Have all the 'clues' which I have assembled added up to a full and coherent story, an outline of *the* explanation or correct philosophical account of forgiveness? Have I told you anything you didn't already know? Well, perhaps not – but then perhaps you only needed to be reminded of what you already knew, anyway. Perhaps the best we can do, in philosophy, *vis-à-vis* forgiveness, is to point out how we play this game, how we – sometimes, apparently – do this amazing, ordinary thing. I have tried to emphasize the '*extraordinariness*' of this 'ordinary' thing.

But in case anyone thinks that any more than that has been achieved, in case one is tempted to think that a distinctive and powerful philosophical understanding of or account of forgiveness has been – could be? – achieved, it is worth remarking bluntly that the kinds of things that I have been led to speak of – a change of heart, an elusive change in one's way of being-in-the-world – are so vague, so untheorizable, that I don't think what I'm saying amounts to anything more than what religious folk have spoken of for centuries when they've said things like, 'Forgiveness is only possible through the grace of God', or 'She must truly be a saint, to have forgiven them for that'. Now, maybe that kind of thing is exactly what we should say; or even, 'Only God can truly forgive'. Just two points:

1). It is not at all obvious that such sentiments as these are *explanations/analyses* at all, as opposed to cover stories (cover-ups) for a lack of explanation/analysis. (Likewise, it is all the same to me whether one says, 'There isn't any such thing as counting to infinity', or 'There's nothing that would count as counting to infinity', or 'Only God can count to infinity'; only provided that whichever of these one chooses to say, it is said (and heard) in the right spirit …)

2). Again, I want to understand forgiveness as a human phenomenon, as something that happens between people, which it seems to me is how the term is overwhelmingly used nowadays (in quite secular contexts), and it's just not going to be good enough in relation to that to *rely upon* concepts of God/divinity.

But it seems to me that the religious version of forgiveness which I have just – *very* schematically – considered offers, too, a clue. The clue is this: perhaps we need to *accept* that there is something truly worth calling mysterious about forgiveness. Not 'supernatural', that never helps,[3] but mysterious nevertheless, by which I mean surprising, *perplexing*, not open to explication in terms other than its own, certainly not in the terms of any academic discipline. Perhaps we need to accept that there are strict limitations on the extent to which any would-be social-scientific or linguistic or philosophical account of certain things that go on between human beings can actually be effective. And if all we can end up saying is, 'Well, it requires a special kind of change of heart … and I can't really tell you in which circumstances that change of heart will or will not take place', then we might as well say, 'It's a mystery; there isn't going to be any successful account of forgiveness of the kind which one naturally wishes to imagine'.

What I have just outlined is in fact the kind of stance that I am inclined to take up (and talk up).

The considerations I have so far adduced might lead someone to conclude that forgiveness is impossible (but just *what* is it that would then be being said to be impossible?), or that it is through and through paradoxical. They might lead someone to conclude that 'forgiveness' is a dead letter in a post-Christian world, as dead as 'taboo' or 'virtue' have elsewhere been argued to be.

I myself am strongly inclined to look for – to see – the order in this human practice, even if its order is far less evident – and far less accountable – than is the order of many other practices. I think that we don't know what we're saying if we assert that forgiveness is impossible, or *literally* supernatural. We have incoherent desires with regard to our words; we want those words to function in ways in which they do not function, while continuing to want them to function in enough of the same old way as to make the label ('forgiveness') fit at all. We incoherently want to say that there is something-which-we-can-make-no-sense-of which is impossible, or possible through supernatural intervention. But if we can really make no sense of it, then even to say (say) that it is impossible is to say too much (I will return to and explain this thought more fully at the conclusion of this chapter).

I think we ought to be humble in the face of some things that people apparently do, things which we cannot get our heads around. I see forgiveness as a human phenomenon. This (important) 'language-game' is played, and without the dubious theoretical assumptions of certain other would-be language-games (water-divining, metaphysical philosophy). But some language-games don't take to *any* kind of theorization or analysis of themselves. I don't say that there is no forgiving, or that the very concept of forgiving is confused; I say that forgiveness is remarkable and rather mysterious, that it happens, if at all, in ways that fit quite poorly with its 'surface grammar' – and that it is rare.

Let me turn to a couple of major objections to my line of thought, to my provisional conclusion here, two objections at least which must be responded to:

'A problem with your account – or non-account – is that you focus too much on the act of forgiveness – and on *the act*

to be forgiven, on the betrayal, or whatever. You ought instead
to focus on the person doing the forgiving and on *the person
to be forgiven*. You ought to separate out the act from the
person and understand that forgiveness is indeed something
that happens between *persons – not* "between actions"!'

There surely is something rather odd or absurd in any
account which talks only of acts being forgiven; I very much
hope that I have not courted such absurdity. Furthermore, I
will not deny that this objection, too, contains a clue – the last
half of its last sentence is surely right and important. But I'm
unhappy with the first half of that sentence. It seems to me very
problematic rigorously to separate act from actor, 'sin' from
'sinner'. If we take this objection seriously, then we must think
of the kind of effect it has radically to divide act from actor,
as, for example, in cases of diminished responsibility in the
courts, or in cases of Dissociative Identity Disorder/Multiple
Personality Disorder: 'It wasn't really *you*, it was your "alter"
personality'. There may be contexts – in particular, specific
legal and medical contexts – in which these are the right things
to say. But I think that it would be extremely unsatisfactory
if our general understanding of forgiveness had to rely upon
such notions. I think that what we need always to keep in
mind is that forgiveness is supposed to be about a-person-
who-*did*-something-*wrong*. You've got to keep the act and
the actor in the frame together. Unless these two are kept,
as it were, *internally related*, unless you keep a notion of the
integrity of the person, unless you can take *that* seriously, then
you're not going to be talking about forgiveness *at all*.

The second objection turns the focus from the 'sinner' more
explicitly to the 'sinned against':

'Maybe you're concentrating too much on the act/person
to be forgiven. Maybe you need to focus on *you*, the person
betrayed, the would-be-forgiver. Maybe you yourself, the
wounded party, is the key here – for isn't the ultimate reason
to forgive because it will yield private spiritual and personal

gain and healing? The resentment, after all, is almost certainly hurting you more than it hurts the wrongdoer.'

This kind of view – that forgiveness is essentially something that you do for yourself – underlies most of the burgeoning forgiveness-as-self-help literature of the present time. Again, though, this line of objection, while popular, and perhaps potentially healthy in asking and saying what forgiveness can do for you rather than only asking what you can do for forgiveness (for God), is highly problematic. To say why, let me turn to Jacques Derrida, the recently deceased French philosopher of Deconstruction. Derrida has said virtually nothing about forgiveness, but I want to invoke his powerful deconstruction of the concept of 'the gift' here. What Derrida says, in essence, is roughly this: If you really look at examples of so-called gift-giving, what you find is that they amount to exchanges, to gifts being 'given' simultaneously or interleaved in time. So, for example, if you are giving x a present, but expecting a 'gift' in return, at least a gift of gratitude or a sense of ongoing indebtedness, then in what sense is it really a *gift* that you have given them? Our ethically imbued perception of what a gift is or should be seems to call out for something beyond that.[4]

A full discussion of these matters would take us too far beyond the present context, into (fascinating) questions of the possibility of altruism and the difficult issue of how and when human behaviour can be 'authentic', 'spontaneous', and/or 'natural'. But I think that – without begging too many questions on these weighty matters – we can say at least this: that what Derrida says of giving can plainly be said, with some real and immediate plausibility, of forgiving. In specific relation to the objection we are considering, how should Derrida's thought be applied? Well, if forgiveness is a gift that one gives essentially to oneself, this seems to short-circuit the presence of the other person altogether. Derrida would surely say that if you are 'giving' the benediction of forgiveness only so as to use the other person to gain something for yourself – for example, a new set of feelings of ease and tranquillity – then you're not really giving a gift at all. If you're forgiving for your own benefit, is that really *forgiveness* at *all*?

This is important enough for it to be worth circling the same terrain with a couple of re-statements: doesn't forgiveness have to be, as it were, essentially other-directed? Doesn't it have to be ... truly a gift, freely *given*? If Derrida is right, then surely the objection to my argument which we have been considering *fails*; and, more generally, support is given to my 'positive' characterization of forgiveness as elusive, mysterious and rare.

The objector might try again, though, roughly as follows: 'Your Derridean "Deconstructionist" argument is all very well; but there remains an ordinary sense in which there is an ordinary practice/language-game of gift-giving. Surely we can and do still talk, quite intelligibly, about giving each other presents at Christmas, for example. That's how our "language-game" is.' And this last point is true. So maybe we shouldn't put *too* much weight on the argument from Derrida. But there remains a response that can be given to the objection, a response which will take us back to the structure of my response to the would-be speech-act-analysis of forgiveness: imagine that you've been given a Christmas present. The following summer, you somehow find yourself asking the giver, 'But have you really given me this present?' What a very bizarre question. Under almost any imaginable circumstances, the answer would probably be something like, 'Well, *of course* – and anyway, what are you talking about, I mean, why are you asking me this, what are you trying to say?'

So, Derrida notwithstanding, there *does* remain a straightforward, ordinary sense in which, once a gift is given, then there you have it. But I want to say, once again, that *forgiveness isn't like that*. This time, imagine that *you* were the perpetrator. It *can* be to the point, if someone made a declaration of forgiveness to you at Christmas-time, say, to ask them, the following summer, perhaps after overhearing an off-colour remark or observing an ongoing pattern of behaviour, the following: 'But have you really forgiven me for doing *y*?'

What, in sum, do I want to say about forgiveness? Let me return you to the first things I did in this chapter. I asked you to imagine a wrong done to you – a deception or betrayal, or even 'just' a deliberate spillage of coffee over you. I didn't ask you to imagine a rape or murder, or a brutalizing deep-set institutionalized racism, still less an extermination. (In the latter cases, there may even be no one left who is in a position to be able to forgive the perpetrators. The most unforgivable vast crimes are those which kill so many that the perpetrators have no one left to whom in good conscience they could go to ask forgiveness ...) But even in the case only of a coffee being spilt over you, or of a deception by a friend, we have found it near-impossible to understand intellectually/philosophically how one could forgive, and what it could mean to do so. I think that most wrongs done to people, not just the most extreme wrongs, *are not forgiven*. They are unforgiven, or they are simply forgotten. Years pass and one forgets the innumerable petty wrongs that remain wrongs that were done to one (and that one did) – usually. And in some *rare* cases, a wrong is remembered and yet forgiven.

How does forgiveness happen? My suggestion is that, in all but a tiny minority of cases, it does not. Either because it is not required, or because it is sidelined by something else happening (e.g. a forgetting, or a practical decision) – or because it just does not. And often, in a relatively short space of time there is no one left who could do the forgiving. (Again: who, now, is well placed to forgive perpetrators of the major genocides of the first half of the twentieth century? It takes enough temerity to fancy oneself well placed even to forgive those who have harmed just one of those nearest and dearest to one.) We are left, perhaps, just wishing desperately that things had been different. But they weren't; they aren't.

And with that thought, we need to return to another moment early in this chapter. I wrote earlier that it would seemingly be straightforward to understand how forgiveness can happen at all, if forgiveness were of the following nature: if the past actually changed, if the deed were literally undone, when forgiveness was sought and granted. Then, I took it, it would be clear why forgiveness was desirable, why it was engaged in – and why it was wonderful. But the scenario I have just sketched is *utter* fantasy. By which I mean: I don't think we have any clear idea of what it would be even to understand such a 'scenario'. What sense can we make, for example, of sentences which speak of the past as subject to change? If the past could be changed, would it any longer be anything we would properly wish to call 'the past'? We have all seen sci-fi films involving 'time travel' 'back' 'into the past' – how many of us, seriously, think we are doing anything other than engaging with a charming illusion of sense – imagining that we imagine something, 'picturing' what is through and through an illusion – when we entertain ourselves by means of such mind-boggling 'scenarios' (such as the utterly absurd scenario of the powerful and highly entertaining *Terminator* films)? Indeed, isn't much of the entertainment derived precisely *from* the utter boggle we experience in watching such films?

We very easily find ourselves with incoherent desires with regard to our words, when we speak of forgiveness as when we speak of time. These incoherent desires lead us to say (incoherent) things like 'Forgiveness is impossible', or 'Forgiveness is incoherent', or 'Forgiveness would be possible if only time travel were possible', or 'You can only travel forward in time', or 'Why shouldn't we be able to travel backwards in time?'

What we ought to say, I think, is that there is *no* way that we can think ourselves into a 'superior' position for comprehending what forgiveness is and how it is possible. And again, let the language here not mislead us – this is not because of an incapacity on our parts. To say 'God alone understands forgiveness; and we forgive through God alone' is, outside, perhaps, of some very specific religious context(s) where it may have its sense, to say as much and as little as saying 'Forgiveness is simply incomprehensible'. But what we must also say, if we are to say anything, it seems, is 'Forgiveness (sometimes) occurs'. This language-game – this interweaving of actions and words – is 'simply', sometimes, played. And most of those times will not end up being times in which, without taking up a controversial political or ethical stance, we can say that the game transparently should not be played, and/or is obfuscatory or *dangerous*.

But perhaps such a stance is appropriate more often than one might like to think. Especially if one is a contemporary liberal or radical westerner. For I want to close this chapter by connecting my thought that, very often, forgiveness of wrongdoers just does not happen (they are unforgiven, or their acts simply forgotten) with my thought that the game of forgiving, and especially the trying to get others to play the game, is frequently dangerous. I want to make the connection via one final more concrete example.

This time, I have in mind not the self-help literature on and 'practice' of, but the *human rights* literature on and 'practice' of forgiveness. Specifically, I have in mind the recent Truth and Reconciliation Commission (TRC) in South Africa. I'm thinking, for instance, of certain moments in the proceedings of that Commission when certain perpetrators of violence seeking (or granted) amnesty would look for physical signs or tokens of forgiveness/reconciliation from the relatives of victims. I felt very uncomfortable witnessing any such moments. I might sum up why, again perhaps following Derrida, by saying this: I don't think that forgiveness is something which can be *forced*. Still less institutionalized.[5]

This is perhaps the cash-value of what might seem to some the mere paradox-mongering which I have engaged in here, in this chapter. If what I am saying here is right, then I think that one has to have pretty serious qualms about the quasi-injunction that emerges not just from forgiveness-as-self-help, and from much contemporary religion, but also from the contemporary 'human rights culture', as manifested, for example, in the TRC. This human rights culture, which has risen to greater and greater prominence over the last twenty years, perhaps not coincidentally with 'the fall of Communism', is something which it is terribly hard to oppose. South Africa's TRC, for instance, seems so noble; and anyway, what other options – practical political possibilities – are there for countries trying to repair themselves and which have given up on goals of revolutionary transformation? Well, my qualms can be put thus: I worry that philosophers, among others, may be being enlisted in trying *to force forgiveness* – this rare, obscure, remarkable thing – and perhaps thus to short-circuit certain necessary processes of justice, of reparation, of politics, of reckoning. If forgiveness is, as I have argued, at *best* partially explicable and uncommonplace, then we ought to be wary of trying to replace retributive and/or reparative justice with 'restorative justice' (the ideal of the TRC) – not least because if I am right, then what the TRC (for instance) is trying to do is very unlikely to actually *work*.

My own belief is that an alternative to the deliberate search for the 'restoration' of humanity and community through forgiveness and reconciliation is at least partially available, and that it is taken to be politically and economically impossible only at the cost of a terrible socio-political – and, one might say, philosophical – gamble. The alternative I have in mind is massive reparations, punitive taxes on those who profited from apartheid, for instance. That might be a true token of repentance – with any luck, it might even lead to some forgiveness!

In supporting such an alternative, even now, I follow one of the TRC's subtlest critics, Mahmood Mamdani:

> By reducing apartheid to its worst perpetrators is not the TRC turning into a rescue operation for [apartheid's] beneficiaries? The alternative I suggest to you, is not to victimise the beneficiaries this time round for that would be revenge, but there is an alternative other than revenge. There is a form of justice other than victor's justice. That alternative is to begin with to get beneficiaries to see their own social responsibility ...

If the Committee were altered thus, then

> It would be a commission whose purpose would be to teach beneficiaries not only of the abuses for which they bear no [direct] personal responsibility but also of the structural injustice of which they have been direct beneficiaries, and therefore bear direct responsibility to redress. And it would be a commission, which would now forefront the notion of justice, not as criminal but as social justice, as the only morally acceptable way of living with a morally unacceptable truth.[6]

What Mamdani's proposal would surely do is to yield some real sense of *justice*. Whereas the call to forgive, whether from Mother Teresa or Desmond Tutu or even Mandela, always risks functioning as a call to preserve the status quo and as a cover-up for the preservation of injustice. Those who have suffered, not unreasonably, want more than to love their ex-enemies; they want a promise of a genuinely more just future, and they want those promises to be delivered on.

Now, of course, the rich and powerful are right to sense – and this again follows from my argument that forgiveness is a tenuous achievement – that no matter how much they democratize or redistribute, there is no guarantee that they will be (or stay) forgiven by those who have suffered. But the cash-value of philosophizing about forgiveness remains, I think, this: a stronger sense of the ethical *and* political risks that are run by the attempted institutionalization and generalization of something less explicable than (say) promising, and rarer even than (say) love. We might then try using a form of words such as the following: that forgiveness, where possible *and appropriate*, is a great ethical act in its own right; it is a renewal of the possibility for life to go on well – even a reparation of a tear in existence. An act of true forgiveness adds something to life; we give something to life with this act.

But if words such as these don't satisfy you, then all the philosophizing in the world will add nothing further except, possibly, to defer the question to ethics and politics – something that must be lived, and will never be 'fully understood', and will never be philosophized into submission.

III Politics

Editor's Introduction

In *The Republic*, Plato is said to have argued for philosophers as ideal rulers of the ideal state. Guided by their knowledge of 'the truth', philosopher kings would be the best dispensaries of the common good. Whether or not this is what Plato 'meant', the idea never had too much positive uptake, in ancient Greece or now. But why not? One easily calls up images of philosophers as either wrinkled ivory-tower fogies out of touch with the common citizenry, or wild-eyed crazies spouting empty polemic. *But why* – isn't there a way for philosophy to contribute to politics?

This section suggests that Plato went wrong in proposing a philosophical elite, a dictatorship of the philosopheriat privileged with a special 'knowledge'. Instead, through looking closely and carefully at assumptions and things taken for granted, appreciating the ways in which our common sense can be bewitched by careful and crafty PR men, etc., philosophy as properly understood *clears the ground* of confusions preventing right action. It stops elites from bamboozling those with less cognitive intelligence or simply less resources than themselves. The way forward, as a result, is left obvious. Thus, philosophy prepares the way for a truly democratic politics, a politics for all.

The first chapter in this section, 'How I learned to love Noam Chomsky' (parts of which were previously published in *Philosophical Writings* and as 'One World' newspaper columns in the *Eastern Daily Press*), discusses modern Orwellianism in such topics as 'the war on terror', 'freedom of choice', etc. and how one philosopher's close looking reveals confusions that allow many political problems to persist. When the functioning of modern propaganda, the propaganda of Bush and Blair and co., is exposed to the cold light of day, then we have already begun to reclaim democracy in its truest sense: rule by the people (rather than rule by an elite that mostly just pretends to enjoy popular support, and that virtually buys its way into power with huge corporate donations). To adapt a metaphor of Wittgenstein's: Chapter 6 exposes the common political lies embedded in our ordinary discourse to the sunlight of critical attention. Thus it stops their growth much as potatoes sprout less in the light than they do if hidden away in a dark cupboard.

The second chapter, '*Rings*, Power, Fear, and Politics' (which contains sections of a book review published in *Philosophical Psychology*) works a bit differently. It is intended to take the reader on a thinking-through of a pervasive political issue: the role of (particularly violent) power in achieving and maintaining security. It explores how some (problematic) presuppositions are played out in a creative imagining of the world – and isn't it the politics of today that *create* the world of tomorrow? – by treating *The Lord of the Rings* as an allegory of paranoia; and it suggests that the attitude of 'leading' politicians in the world today – of Bush and Blair and Bin Laden alike – is a fundamentally paranoid one. Non-state terrorism and 'the war on terror' are both *counterproductive* ways of attempting to achieve safety for oneself and one's followers. In short, Chapter 7 sees a much-loved work of literature and film through a political, psychological and philosophical lens, in order to help us get clearer about what it is to be genuinely safe, suggesting that he who lives by the sword will always fear (by) the sword. Which may be even worse than dying (by it).

In some way, every chapter in each section of this book is political. What is the particular value of these two chapters, then? By addressing the subject directly, rather than as the consequence of some other commitment (as with environmentalism in Chapter 1), these essays show 'politics' to be a body more of misconceptions than 'platforms', ideologies or theories. The aim is to use philosophy to clear the way for a politics that can, instead, be a way of expressing ourselves and taking power: not the power of threats, violence, lies and linguistic distortions, but of people running their own affairs.

6 How I Learned to Love Noam Chomsky

This essay is a practical exercise in applying the thought of Wittgenstein to human affairs – to language, to politics. I shall lay out as we go reasons for thinking that a successful approach to these matters cannot consist in the construction of theories or the pronouncement of theses. An effective (Wittgensteinian) 'political philosophy' is going to have to look very different from almost any political philosophy that we are used to. For starters, it will avoid theorizing by working always with 'examples' of the actual use of language in context(s). We must *look* at human affairs, and then we will see.

Is that obscure? If so, then perhaps what I am getting at can begin to be better illustrated via the following quote from Wittgenstein: 'What *we* do is to bring words back from their metaphysical to their everyday use'.[1]

It is precisely this, a careful observation of politics and a watchful stewardship of language employed in political endeavours that, I contest, has allowed Noam Chomsky[2] to establish an international fame and success as a public intellectual. Look, for instance, at his deep opposition to intellectual elitism in matters of political theory and practice, and his deep suspicion of those who would be (in policy-making or in providing the kind of background of academic respectability that policy-makers like and eventually need) quasi-scientific '*experts*' regarding political and historical matters. He mocks the need for grand theories in the political and historical sphere, suspecting that all such theories and models are rackets for the obscuring of truths which are quite within the grasp of any moderately well-informed citizen.

Instead, he simply *describes* what is happening/has happened and endeavours systematically to debunk and unmask those who would give false or misleading descriptions, either directly in their own interests or in the interests of those with power over them, or (more commonly) simply as part of their job, as part of an in-place and functioning system (but a system which we may adjudge overall to be 'dysfunctional' and/or unjust). He is especially concerned at the forms this takes in recent times, where, as he suggests (in the tradition of Orwell), it takes the form, among other things, of a hypostatization of language into a less direct character, into manners of speaking which are less 'uncomfortable' and challenging.

But these remarks are not intended to be evocative of a grand Chomskian political theory – there is none such, only pragmatic common sense and vision and a lot of information (and a smattering of humanistic Anarchist ethical and political principle).[3] The way to understand Chomsky's politics is inevitably in concrete cases. Most notably, perhaps, in the way he attempts to unmask the corruption of the very language we speak, corruption which often seems functionally to occur in order to render it harder than it would otherwise be for ordinary people to grasp what is happening to them or to others.

What do I mean by 'corruption' here? Let us look briefly at some examples. One of Chomsky's methods is simply to take a bit of contemporary news-speak, present us with it, and re-contextualize it to the point that we realize how bizarre it truly is. His paper on 'Problems of Population Control' in a major collection of his articles, *Deterring Democracy*, yields some of many possible exemplifications of this.

The paper begins by citing the *Wall Street Journal*'s headline at the time when there was first talk of a post-Cold-War 'peace dividend' – the *Journal* decided that in fact what we were now seeing arrive was the 'Unsettling specter of Peace'. Chomsky simply allows us to notice how this figuration of peace, as the spectre now haunting Europe and America, can only make sense if one is pursuing the interests of a narrowly defined set of groups (e.g. weapons producers, some economic planners) who do not have the obvious attitude to superpower peace – that of sighing with relief. Chomsky goes on to argue that the approach of this 'spectre' renders it advisable for these particular groups to look for an alternative method of channelling the population's aspirations and fears, now that the threat of the Communists is no longer plausible or relevant. He finds that this alternative has been found in part in 'the Drug War' (it is now pretty clearly done in 'the war on terror') and goes on to suggest some of the manners in which this diversion of attention is fostered, by means, for instance, of focusing on the threat to Third World 'democracies' purportedly posed by drug-trafficking (and by the supposed complicity of leftist guerillas with narco-traffickers), though not, supposedly, by certain other factors (by the actions of the American and British governments, say):

The naive might ask why we [America] fail to exercise our right of intervention in South Korea, Indonesia ... There is no inconsistency, however. These countries are committed to 'democracy' in the operative meaning of the term: unchallenged rule by elite elements ... that generally respect the interests of US investors, with appropriate forms for occasional ratifications by segments of the public. When these conditions are not satisfied, intervention is legitimate to restore democracy.

To take the fashionable case of the 1980s; Nicaragua under the Sandinistas was a 'totalitarian society' (Sec. of State James Baker) ... where we must intervene massively to assure that elites responsive to US interests prevail as elsewhere in the region. Colombia, in contrast, is a democracy with a 'level playing field', in current jargon, since these elements rule with no political challenge. A closer look at Colombia ... provides further insight into what counts as 'democracy'. In Colombia, the *New York Times* informs us, courageous people threatened by 'violence from cocaine gangs' are struggling 'to preserve democratic normalcy'. The reference [to 'courageous people'] is not to peasants, union leaders, or advocates of social justice and human rights who face

the violence of the military and the oligarchy. And crucially, democratic normalcy has never been threatened by the fact that the
two parties that share political power are 'two horses [with] the
same owner' (former President [of Colombia] A.L. Michaelsen) –
not exactly a circumstance unfamiliar to us. Nor does a problem
arise from the actual conditions of this 'democratic normalcy'.
Death squads have killed about 1000 members of the one party
not owned by the oligarchy (the Patriotic Union, UP) since its
founding in 1985, leaving the unions and popular organizations
with no meaningful political representation. These death squads
dedicated to extermination of 'subversives' are in league with the
security forces (Amnesty International). An official government
inquiry made public in 1983 found that over a third of members
of paramilitary groups engaged in political killings and other
terror were active-duty officers, a pattern that continues up to
the present, along with alliances with drug dealers, according to
human rights inquirers ...[4]

'America's historic purpose' and its 'yearning for democracy'
are, so we are told by the mainstream media,[5] not threatened by
these humdrum and myriad violations of what would and do
appear to a competent user of the language to be the most basic
features of ... *democracy*. The misuse of the English language
(in its popular and uncorrupted sense) that is being practised
upon us – that is evident, for instance, in the nested *New York
Times* quote – is part of the context of the violations of decency
and humanity that are obvious in much US policy towards
Latin America. Chomsky is in the business of sarcastically
deconstructing and unmasking the kind of linguistic corruption
that is in play when words are thus abused. He is attempting
to lead his readers to see the nonsense latent in theoretical-
propagandistic discourses that have been presented to us as
obvious truths (or unquestionable frameworks).

Another of Chomsky's deservedly effectual rhetorical
strategies, besides exposing the dubious and 'technical' uses of

words operative in the media (and in parts of the academy), is to call features of (e.g.) the American polity by names which are usually reserved for what 'America' is fighting against, in order to *highlight the 'technical'* – aberrant, extraordinary – *nature of these names' use by the media, government, etc.* Thus, in 'Problems of Population Control', he speaks of 'the Washington Connection'[6] (cf. 'the French Connection') – of the trafficking in illegal drugs to raise money for illegal covert operations (and also of the facilitation of the (legal) export of chemicals that the government has overwhelming evidence to believe will be used to make illegal drugs) – and he speaks more generally of the 'huge narcotrafficking operation'[7] run by the American government (by virtue, under the banner of 'free trade', of its forcing foreign countries to accept its tobacco exports, even when they have laws which would forbid this)!

These methods of Chomsky's are summed up perhaps most effectively in his short and deliberately populist tract, *What Uncle Sam Really Wants*:

WAR IS PEACE. FREEDOM IS SLAVERY. IGNORANCE IS STRENGTH.

The terms of political discourse typically have two meanings. One is the dictionary meaning, and the other is a meaning that is useful for serving power – the doctrinal meaning ...

[T]ake *'free enterprise'*, a term that refers, in practice, to a system of public subsidy and private profit, with massive governmental intervention in the economy to maintain a welfare state for the rich. In fact, in acceptable usage, just about any phrase containing the word 'free' is likely to mean something like the opposite of its actual meaning ...

[Or take] 'special interest' ... The well-oiled Republican PR systems of the 1980s regularly accused the Democrats of being the party of the special interests: women, labor, the elderly, the young, farmers – in short, the general population ...The Democrats plaintively retorted that they were not the party of the special interests: they served the national interest too. That was correct, but their problem has been that they lack the single-minded class consciousness of their Republican opponents. The latter are not confused about their role as representatives of the owners and managers of society ...

To make sense of political discourse, it's necessary to give a running translation into English, decoding the doublespeak of the media, academic social scientists and the secular priesthood generally. Its function is not obscure: the effect is to make it impossible to find words to talk about matters of human significance in a coherent way. We can then be sure that little will be understood about how our society works and what is happening in the world – a major contribution to *democracy*, in the PC sense of the word.[8]

At best, all that one will be able to *trust*, in this process of trying to look and see how one's society is, behind the smoke and mirrors of politically 'metaphysical uses' – i.e. propagandistic abuses – of language, is one's own linguistic competence/performance (one's being a master of a language-in-use). These ought always to be the starting points for any proposed extensions of the use of terms for particular purposes. (Chomsky appeals to nothing else – not, for instance, to empirical fieldwork or to arcane political theory.)

Any technical terms being used in (for instance) what academics call 'political science', Chomsky's position makes clear, need to be justified. Otherwise they stand vulnerable to the charge of not reflecting the self-understandings of the people upon whom the technical terms are being deployed, of substituting instead a superstructure of uses of terms and established presumptions and maxims which will tend, for political and practical reasons, in general only to serve the interests of career-builders in political science, in government planning, etc. And of serving the illusion that our systems of governance and polity in the contemporary West/North are pretty open, free and democratic – while ensuring that these structures remain in practice astonishingly closed and tipped towards the support of corporate and elite power and profits.

And so: Chomsky shows us how we need to and can resist the transformation of our language into something it ought not to be. In his highly practical and non-theoretical political and historical work, he resists the turning of our ordinary language into a replacement for it both technical *and* emotive. And he resists especially the *obscuring* of this turning – the obscurantist failure to admit that the use, for instance, of the binary opposition 'special interest' vs 'public interest' in the US media today is a technical use not reflecting our ordinary or common-sense understanding of these terms, *and* a use furthermore evidently intended (to judge by its 'judicious' deployment on the political Right) to have an emotive effect (i.e. to get us to like tanks rather than people, etc. …).

It would be no exaggeration to say that the picture we find in the language of the modern media is one that tends *to hold us captive* and that fosters an inchoate set of assumptions that are hard to resist because they are so repeatedly implied and 'gently' drummed into us, such that they become the 'received wisdom' not only of our pundits and journalists and politicians and think-tanks and academics, but also of all of us, unless we are very vigilant. I use the word 'inchoate' in the above sentence deliberately, because, rather than being false, many of these assumptions are literally absurd or nonsensical. How could it be, for instance, that 'the public interest' had hardly anything to do with the actual interests (as perceived and comprehended in their guts and in the daily realities of their lives) of the public?! Many of the 'technical' usages of terms in media/academic political discourse have become so perverted that they simply are metaphysical/nonsensical as they stand.

Consider a few more of my current examples, with the Chomskian insights (if this essay has provided any) now at our disposal:

1) Terrorism

In its true meaning, 'terrorism' refers to the terrorizing of people by other people in order to achieve political or military aims. But 'terrorism', in its propagandistic meaning, widespread in the 'Newspeak' of the popular press and of the Bush-Blair-Olmert triumvirate, refers only to hopeless attempts by the desperate and the powerless to achieve their aims by means of scaring civilian populations. Bush-Blair-Olmert refer to Al-Qaida and Hamas as 'terrorists', but would be incredulous at the suggestion that they themselves might be seen as terrorists, although it is obviously true that they employ methods of terror. The 'coalition' in Iraq, for instance, used 'daisy-cutter' bombs and fuel-based incendiaries, weapons more devastating than those used in the terror-bombings of London and Dresden in World War Two. Do you think that the soldiers of Iraq's army, or the hundreds of thousands of civilians who have been killed or seriously injured by 'our' coalition in Iraq, have been anything other than terrified and terrorized by the onslaught unleashed upon them?

The state of Israel was founded by means of terrorism – Menachem Begin, one of Olmert's predecessors as prime minister – was a terrorist with the Stern Gang. Ariel Sharon – Olmert's immediate predecessor and political mentor – followed in his footsteps when, as a general in the Israeli Army, he permitted the war crime of massacring the inhabitants of the Sabra and Shatila refugee camps in Lebanon. But our mainstream press and our political leaders do not allow these things to be respectably said. They refuse to admit that state terrorism, such as that of Bush, Blair and Olmert has killed and terrorized FAR more people in the last few years than non-state terrorists ever have. (We in the peace movement are vilified when we portray such leaders as state sponsors of terrorism – although that is precisely what they are.)

2) Democracy

In the true meaning of the term, 'democracy' means 'government by the people'. But at the hands of the propagandists who dominate our media and the major political parties, 'democracy' in effect becomes domination of the people by the rich and powerful. True democracy would mean that we were seriously involved in deciding the vital questions of our time: questions such as how to combat global warming, or how to organize our transportation systems. As it is, all we get is the right to mark a box on a ballot paper once every four or five years – and the politicians we then elect are free to ignore both our voices and international law. As Marx once remarked, 'in Britain citizens are "free" for one day every five years'. In any case, most of the politicians we are permitted to choose between barely even disagree with each other: for example, all three main political parties in Britain now support globalized capitalism so unreservedly that they all favour further privatization, yet more road-building and the giving up of yet more of our remaining freedoms and rights to patently undemocratic bodies such as the General Agreement on Tariffs and Services and the World Trade Organization. Only on the fringes, in organizations such as the Green Party or the Scottish Socialist Party, can one actually find a different point of view.

We are told that 'the coalition' is bringing 'democracy' to Iraq – but democracy would mean, for instance, the right of Iraq to control its own oil supplies, and the right to its own foreign policy. Yet the USA has already privatized Iraq's oil industry, for the benefit of American oil companies and unaccountable multinationals; and the USA will maintain permanent military bases in Iraq whether the Iraqis like it or not.

3) Strong

Being strong, in truth, means such things as being willing to take risks for peace. Whereas the propagandistic press and establishment politicians perpetrate the myth that being strong means always being self-righteous, engaging in macho posturing (like landing fighter-jets on aircraft carriers, or shouting through bullhorns on the rubble of the World Trade Center) and lusting for revenge.

Bush-Blair are in truth so weak that they cannot bear governments in the Middle East that they do not control; and so weak that they are not prepared to admit the truth that, as is now (at least) quite well known, that the 'coalition' made a dreadful mistake in their claims about Iraq having WMDs. Yet Bush-Blair spend much of their time beating the drum that they are 'strong' leaders.[9]

4) Patriotism

Too often, patriotism doesn't give us any real community. Instead, it gives us only a mythical sense of belonging, a sense that can then be exploited by unscrupulous leaders. Too often, the 'leaders of the free world' use and abuse patriotism to try to get away with murder; isn't this obvious in the way that politicians and generals (do and have always done) *twist* love of country so that it turns into hate for certain foreigners? (It is hard to have any enthusiasm for the flag when that flag has far too often thoughtlessly been waved – in our name – over the bodies of dead foreigners.)

It cannot be right to say 'We should not speak against war,

when our troops are fighting', if what they are fighting in is
an immoral war (that kills, increasingly, them and others). It
cannot be right to say 'My country right or wrong'. That kind
of disgraceful attitude is exactly what led to Hitlerism[10] – and
more recently, in the USA, to the appallingly authoritarian
'Patriot Act' (introduced as a response to the events of 11
September 2001) which virtually abolishes free speech and
'habeas corpus'. Would a true patriot support the destruction
of the very liberties for which the people have fought so
hard, the very liberties that make one's country truly *worth*
defending?

*   *   *

With (even just) individual terms recontextualized in this
way, the whole of mainstream political speech comes to seem
foolish. Consider the old New Labour slogan we've heard little
of recently: 'Tough on crime, tough on the causes of crime'.
When exposed to a Chomsky-style critique, this seemingly
coherent and understandable language, too, begins to break
down in the face of the actual politics of the issue.

For instance, one reason people resort to crime is that
they are poor in an individualistic society which appears
above all to value wealth, because they are not encouraged
to value neighbours and strangers. Being 'tough on crime',
then, is pointless unless one is *actually* prepared to be tough
on crime's causes. It's pointless tackling the symptoms while
ignoring the underlying disease. We need what Blair-Bush
and the host of empowered embedded corporate interest is
reluctant to countenance: redistribution of wealth. What sense
of community can someone feel living in socially deprived
parts of the industrialized world with relatively well-off total
strangers from, say, thousand-acre ranches in Texas or million-
pound flats in London? Two worlds collide, as they did, for
example, when those who were able fled New Orleans ahead

of the onslaught of Hurricane Katrina and then watched on television those who weren't – watched them either die, or suffer (and still suffer) terribly.

If western powers fought a war on poverty, and gave people shared goals to believe in, crime would fall drastically. That would be: getting tough on the causes of crime. Without so doing, being 'tough on crime' *just* means being authoritarian and harsh.

Now what about looking at terrorist crime? If we were going to be 'Tough on terrorism, tough on the causes of terrorism', what would we do differently? Well, we might start by acknowledging (as is done, or at least is begun, in 1) above) where our own country takes part in terrorism. Remember 'Shock and Awe'? Remember the systematic terrorization – the torture – of prisoners in Abu Ghraib and Guantanamo, and more recently the shameful photos of British squaddies found guilty of humiliating and torturing Iraqi civilians? Remember the capricious month-long slaughter (in 2006) of Lebanese civilians and destruction of civilian infrastructure from which that country is yet to recover? Say no more.

Next, we might look deeply to see what turns someone into a non-state terrorist (e.g. a suicide-bomber). What drives people to such despair that they turn themselves into human bombs? Maybe the grinding poverty suffered by most people in the non-western world. Maybe feeling that there is something hypocritical in the West's insistence that we (including Israel) can have nuclear WMDs, but 'if you people ever try to get your hands on WMDs, we will annihilate you'. Maybe the West's propping up of human-rights-abusing regimes across the globe, provided that their leaders are willing to do our bidding and sell us their oil. Maybe a searing sense of injustice at the seemingly endless US military presence in the Middle East; at the killing of a million Iraqis by US/UK sanctions in the 1990s, and of hundreds of thousands more since March 2003; above all, at the vicious occupation of Palestine by the (US-sponsored) Israeli army. Maybe it is understandable, then, why ordinary people, no different at birth from you or I, become 'terrorists'. If you'd been brought up in a refugee camp, seen your parents humiliated daily, been deprived of economic opportunity and given no effective non-violent outlet for your sense of injustice, maybe you too would have despaired enough to strap on a bomb, especially given the thought that doing so created even the slightest chance to save from the same frustration your younger siblings or their children (or your own).

The truth is sometimes uncomfortable: it is our (Britain's and the USA's) unjust foreign policies – crucially, our propping up of the illegal Israeli occupation of Gaza, the West Bank, etc. – which are a pre-eminent cause of non-state terrorism. If global society fought a war on poverty, injustice and oppression, terrorist crime would fall drastically. That would be: being tough on the causes of terrorism.

Examples such as the one above, and Chomsky's applied common-sense analysis of political discourse, to be properly understood, must be seen as attacking not just certain linguistic formulations – certain verbal strings – but perhaps the very notion of rhetoric (at least insofar as it is applied to contemporary politics) itself. Another example should highlight this strong understanding of Chomskian linguistic-politico sensitivity: we are regularly being told about the 'progress' being made in Iraq. We have been told about this progress virtually since the invasion began; but what if Britain or the USA were Iraq?[11] What would comparing the rhetoric in this way do to our conception of the 'progress' that has been made?

* * *

Well, the population of Britain is two and a half times that of Iraq. Much more for the USA. Violence killed at least 2,000

Iraqis over the last month, the equivalent of 5,000 Britons. What if 5,000 Britons had died in aerial bombardments, machine-gun spray and rocket attacks over the last month? That's more than died in the thirty years of Northern Ireland's 'Troubles', and almost double the number of Americans who perished in the 11 September attack ... every month! (Imagine the attack on the World Trade Center repeating itself *twice* EVERY MONTH!)

What if the 'Westminster village' or New York's Greenwich Village were constantly taking mortar fire? And what if almost everyone in there considered it suicidally dangerous to go over to the South Bank or to New Jersey? What if reporters for all the major non-English-speaking media were in effect trapped inside five-star hotels in London or Chicago, wholly dependent on native 'stringers' to know what was happening in East Anglia or the greater Midwest? What if the only time they ventured out was if they could be 'embedded' in army patrols?

There are at least 30,000 guerillas in Iraq engaged in concerted acts of violence. What if there were private armies totalling 75,000 to 100,000 men, armed with machine-guns and mortar launchers, hiding out in urban areas all over the two countries? What if they completely controlled Hartlepool, Winchester, Leicester, Manchester, Sheffield and Peterborough, or Philadelphia, St Louis, San Fransisco or (what's left of) New Orleans such that national army troops and local police could not enter those cities? What if, during the past two years, Britain's Attorney General, the American Secretary of State and the Queen herself had all been assassinated? What if all the cities of Britain and America were wracked by a crime wave, with hundreds or thousands of murders and kidnappings in each major city every year?

What if the US Air Force routinely (I mean daily or weekly) bombed Camden, Soho, Moss Side and Mile Cross, or if the RAF dropped 500-pound bombs anywhere in the five boroughs of New York purporting to target 'safe houses' of 'criminal gangs', but inevitably killing a lot of children and little old ladies?

What if, from time to time, the American army besieged Camden and Mile Cross and the precincts of Canterbury Cathedral, killing hundreds of armed members of the 'Christian Soldiers'? What if entire platoons of the Christian militia were holed up in Highgate Cemetery and were bombarded by US Air Force warplanes daily, these bombings destroying hundreds of famous graves? What if the Archbishop of Canterbury had to call for a popular march of tens of thousands of Christian believers to converge at Canterbury Cathedral to stop the Americans from damaging it further through their bombing raids?

What if Billy Graham were folded directly into the political discourse as a negotiator because of his sway over 'insurgent' loyalists? What if there were a Billy-army, better outfitted than British soldiers, who initiated a major battle and seized sizeable territory in the area outside downtown Washington DC every year, only to be bought off and retreat back to hovels in Georgetown awaiting next year's opportunity for a power grab?

What if there were virtually no non-military air or rail travel? What if many roads were highly dangerous, especially the M1 from the North Circular to the Watford Gap, or Interstate I-95 from Philadelphia to Washington? If you used them, you were gambling with your life, at risk of carjacking, or 'collateral damage' from coalition troops' guns.

What if no one outside Westminster or the Capitol District had electricity for more than 12 hours a day? What if electricity went off at unpredictable times, causing factories to grind to a halt and air conditioning to fail in the middle of intense summer heatwaves?

What if oil rigs in the Gulf of Mexico were bombed and disabled at least monthly? What if unemployment hovered around 40 per cent, and in inner city areas was nearer 80 per cent? What if veterans of the Ulster Freedom Fighters and ex-police officers who had been sacked for their 'shoot to kill' policy against Irish Catholics were brought in by Britain to run the American government and the army, on the theory that we need tough men in charge at times of crisis?

What if the British people consistently said in opinion polls that they were more scared of American occupiers than of any guerillas, and that they simply wanted the occupying forces to leave now – and yet American leaders kept insisting that the people welcomed them and that anyway they were only staying at the invitation of the new 'sovereign' British government? What if Portuguese and Italian leaders constantly maintained that nevertheless freedom, democracy and peace were just around the corner?

*   *   *

Of course one may object in defence of the old saw that this chaos is an improvement on what was there before, the violent caprice of a brutal dictator. Or one may claim, following the horribly pedantic rhetoric of Condoleeza Rice et al, that these are simply the 'birth pangs' of the new 'freedom' being born into the Middle East. One would do well, if clinging to the first, to review the charges for which Saddam Hussein has recently stood trial and for which he was hanged: whose body count, whose inflicted suffering, whose mass grave stuffing is more abhorrent? The lights stayed on (except, of course, when shutting them off helped the exterminations of his opponents in, say, Kurdistan or the south), at least, under Saddam Hussein. Moreover, one should recall that when Saddam was doing all this utterly heinous stuff, the British and the US governments were his staunchest supporters ...

One clinging to the second objection must acknowledge that such bold talk and predictions are not logic but hope (which, as we know, often persists in the face of overwhelming evidence to the contrary). Of course, such a person can always just wait ... and count the body bags.

*   *   *

I hope that these examples may be of some use in understanding the absolutely fundamental importance of Chomsky's work, in his pitiless defacing of the deception of political rhetoric. He has been an inspiration to those – such as 'Medialens', the Glasgow Media Group and the anti-war movement across the world – who seek to overcome propaganda and, truly, give peace a chance. I hope that the analyses above will make it seem a little less odd to say that I LOVE this great dissident Noam Chomsky who, in his political and historical work, brings words like 'American' and 'national interest' and 'Communist' and 'conservative' and 'victory' and 'freedom fighter' and 'truth' back *from their metaphysical to their everyday uses*. It seems to me that it is true (applied political) philosophy to do what Chomsky does: to look at the illusions (not simple falsehoods) that are perpetrated upon us (*and* that we perpetrate upon ourselves and others) when language goes on holiday ...

... or is sent to war.

7 *Rings*, Power, Fear and Politics[1]

There is a strong current trend of mining recent 'children's books' for parallels with the greatest literature in (at least) the western tradition. But as much as the impulse to find a successor to this canon in the *Harry Potter* series may be stymied – thwarting attempts to analyse timeless greatness (versus, perhaps, simply commercial potential) out of those books (their success in spurring on adolescent literacy aside) – I do not think this impulse to be itself deeply problematic at all. I think there is much to support an argument for the historical greatness of at least one epic series often seen as most appropriate for children: *The Lord of the Rings*. For *The Lord of the Rings* is a work which offers truly rich veins to be mined: philosophic, psychological and political insights, which sometimes attain the same depth as the insights of other great 'quest' epics, such as the Arthurian legends and Homer's epics.[2] It may seem absurd to credit this 'children's book' with such ambitions, but it is difficult otherwise to escape the question of what explains the enduring and quite vast appeal of *The Lord of the Rings*. How and why is this book – which has been in wide readership now for over fifty years and was just recently made into three fabulously successful and (in my view) deeply impressive films by Peter Jackson – able to touch parts that other works in its class cannot reach? What does this (possibly) seemingly *jejune* tale of swash-and-buckle have to teach us about our own time, our own politics?

In brief: *The Lord of the Rings* is in my view best read as an allegory of madness and the devastating consequences of madness when it lies behind political power. It argues that the desire to achieve safety through the acquisition of power over one's fellows, one's life, one's experiences, leads only to self-defeating fantasies, and that the hard route of ordinary 'faith', and renunciation of any quick-fix fantasy of safety, is the only route that will succeed. The methods for dealing with extreme anxiety – anxiety that makes one desperate for safety – explored by *The Lord of the Rings* are: 1). a retreat away from the consensual world and into the perceived safety concealed deep inside the mind, a journey to the edge of psychosis symbolized by the putting on of the Ring; 2). a giving in, symbolized by the possibility of giving away the Ring to Sauron (the Lord of the Rings) and his surrogates; 3). a breaking of the power of the temptation to 'give in', symbolized, above all, by the dissolving of the Ring in the fires from whence it was forged; and 4). the contemplation of 1). through 3). enacted for example by a 'philosophical' reading of *The Lord of the Rings*, or at least its careful and thoughtful reading by a philosophically inclined reader. Tolkien's book argues for 3). and 4). and against 1). and 2). and in the course of doing so it dramatizes and indeed investigates many philosophical issues of intense related interest.

I believe, then, that *The Lord of the Rings* not only expounds but also genuinely extends our understanding of those dynamics of human thought which are 'psychopathology'. It has certainly extended mine. Right from the sense of strangeness – the sudden need to scrutinize and to hide – which constitutes a rising tide of perplexing open-ended anxiety, of 'schizy' trouble as soon as the Ring makes its presence felt at the start of the story, all the way to the tragic departure of the ring-bearers from the consensual everyday world, at the story's end.

Let us start our exploration (of what I allege is Tolkien's and Jackson's exploration of these matters) with a near-truism about *The Lord of the Rings*: that the Ring is power, that power corrupts (unless perhaps it is founded in tradition, integrity, honesty and 'democratically'-earned respect), and that absolute power corrupts absolutely. This is often supposed to be the teaching of Tolkien, and I do not deny that it is. But how does power corrupt? Merely because you can do more of 'whatever you like', the more powerful you become? No; that is true, but shallowly so. *Also*, and more crucially, because as your power grows, so the fear others have of you grows, and so their incentive to rein you in or overthrow you grows, *and so your* sense *of vulnerability grows* and your sense of your security – your reliable, *felt* power – shrinks. Personal power is therefore like a drug – larger and larger quantities of it are required just to keep you at the same level of security. And eventually even the largest possible quantity is not enough.

The deep truth in the truism that all power corrupts and absolute power corrupts absolutely is that there is an in-built tendency in (what we know as) power to corrupt the mind. *Power held in the hands of an individual breeds in its possessor[3] a corrosive sense of lack of sufficient power.*

The One Ring is apparently an apotheosis of power. It stands thereby as a metaphor for the truism about power and corruption that we have been discussing. And it does. But we might start to wonder if that is the whole story, in looking a little closer at the texture of *The Lord of the Rings*, by asking about what powers the One Ring *actually* has.

It undoubtedly has the power to make the wearer invisible. This power, which is the one power of the 'Ring of Gyges' in Plato's fertile myth, is a wonderful seeming-guarantor of safety to the wearer, and a possible jumping-off point for him to seem (at least to himself) to move beyond good and evil. One can hit people and run away, etc. (see p. 112 below), without being caught – and perhaps without even being subject to shame. There is at least no apparent rise in colour in the cheeks *of one who is invisible*.

The heretical question I want to raise about the One Ring in *The Lord of the Rings*, a question that I think sparks considerable interest once it is thought through and is therefore at *least* worthy of consideration *for the sake of argument*, is whether it actually has *any* OTHER positive powers than this one (i.e. conferring invisibility). In the films, for instance, we seem to see the One Ring effecting some real, magically violent power only in the distant semi-mythic past, on Sauron's hand, just before it is cut from him by Isildur. (And even this power is much less than, for example, the magic wielded by Gandalf on the battlefields of the Deeping-coomb and of the Pelennor Fields.)

The *only* clearly demonstrated power of the One Ring is its wonderful power to make the wearer invisible. To allow him *to retreat from the consensual world.*

The Ring thereby protects its wearer; that much we know. But what *happens* when the wearer protects himself by withdrawing from the consensual reality of those around him, by becoming invisible?

He enters a twilight world, a lifeworld devoid of life – except for the threat of the half-life that, surprisingly, lurks there. For here is the strange thing: when one seeks safety, when one a gains an idea of where one wants to be that is not where one is right now, when one seeks inviolability – withdrawal from harm – through the power of the One Ring, one finds it at best only very temporarily.[4] The desire for absolute safety leads in fairly short order to the desire to take off the Ring and even to give it away to the 'evil monsters' who seek it – because it is *awful* 'there', in what one thought (what one *desperately* hoped) would be a *safe* 'place'.

When you put on the Ring, you do not (except very briefly) achieve what you want, namely safety, a place where you can be *lord* and master. Where you alone rule. For sure, you are no longer in the world with people. But it is not that you have neatly withdrawn from that world to another place, or to private seclusion within it. Your *whole world* changes. The change is not a coming into possession of a power that you formerly lacked in the same old world; nor is it finding a hiding-place in that world. Rather, the very form of your being-in-the-world is fundamentally altered.[5] In Jackson's brilliant vision, the twilight existence of the 'Ring-world' is qualitatively and not merely quantitatively different from our own.

So: what quickly happens to one in 'Ring-world' is that one comes to feel much less alone than one had hoped to be by escaping from the gaze and scrutiny of others. Crucially, this world is a (non-)world beset almost instantly with paradox. Frodo comes to feel powerfully and horribly *watched*. There is a gaze upon him even in the would-be-utter privacy of his place of retreat, his place of great control, a monstrous gaze that grows and grows until it threatens to pinpoint and utterly know and presumably destroy him. His feeling of vulnerability in the consensual world prompted a flight to a place of invisibility, but he quickly feels even more unsafe there than he felt in the (dangerous) situation that he was in in the real world.

This is, I think, an extremely powerful and even (painfully) beautiful allegorical depiction of the actual nature of the paranoia and mental disturbedness that accompanies, that necessarily constitutes, the quest for (particularly violent) power (though the power to turn invisibile is not necessarily violent, it is, as I suggest on p. 110 above, at least potentially violent, or subject to the temptation to violence).

The Ring has prodigious 'negative' powers – the power to make you *mad* with craving or with terror (we see this personified in the Ring-wraiths; they are fully corrupted by the craving for the ring(s) of power; all they do is seek;[6] they *are* craving)[7] and/or the power to make you *mad* with fear. *Does* it have the positive powers alleged for it (except for that symbolically essential power of rendering invisible to the ordinary eye)? We never see any of them, at least not in the present of the action of the story.[8]

At any rate, it should by now be clear that if the One Ring is properly understood as the apotheosis of power, then that power is at best not a desirable one, or one that provides only the appearance of safety or dominion over others. Is *The Lord of the Rings* then about power and its corrupting effects, or is it about the *fantasy* of achieving safety through power and about the self-defeating effects of that fantasy?

* * *

To explore this issue more fully, let us engage with the question of why the power of the Ring gets stronger the closer one gets to Mordor. Why *does* Frodo's task keep getting harder?

My suggestion is this: the closer one gets to destroying the Ring, to the genesis of it and its power that might also be its doom, the heavier it gets, because the closer you come to feeling fully safe in your ordinary existence, and thus to letting go for ever of the method (the magical talisman) that promised/promises you a special safety and dominion, the less safe you are tempted to feel. This is a paradox that one has to live through. The Ring connotes and promises the permanent possibility of invisibility, inviolability to blame and shame and punishment, a wonderful withdrawal. Giving up this refuge *once and for all*, which is inevitably the meaning of casting the Ring into the fires of Mount Doom, is thus a weighty – a terrifying – prospect. Giving up the fantasy of absolute security involves overcoming one's terror of facing a life without any guarantees.

This is why, in light of all of the other action happening concomitantly with Frodo's slow toil towards Mount Doom, *The Lord of the Rings* remains Frodo's story. Ordinary life, companionship and the building of trust (including, crucially, in oneself), achieved not through the more extraordinary version of these that is ideologically involved in being a warrior, are the hardest of all the challenges faced by the epic's characters. The ordinary semi-private task of not giving up where the not-giving-up in the face of great temptation is a daily – almost continuous – occurrence. And where one is deliberately going to face one's greatest terror.

My philosophical claim, then, is that in the sense in which Frodo and all of us fear touching bottom, our fear is groundless – except as self-fulfilling fear. *There is no compelling reason to believe* that anyone cannot come back from the temptation to moral nihilism, from profound selfishness, even from a desperate or desolate withdrawal from life altogether.

Witness here Sam's words to Frodo inside Mount Doom.[9] As Sam sees Frodo hesitating to cast the Ring into the lava, he calls out to him in desperation, 'What are you waiting for? JUST LET IT GO!' Once the Ring has fallen into the lava, but has not yet been destroyed, Frodo hangs on by his fingertips – and still feels the attraction of the Ring pulling him down. Sam's words to him, as he leans down to offer Frodo his hands to pull him to safety?: 'DON'T LET GO! *REACH!*' Reach out, even with your bloodied, disfigured hand. Here, in this movement from 'Let go!' to 'Don't let go!', Sam is presenting to Frodo perhaps the only possible *cure* for the desperate search for guranteed safety and security: a sort of twofold faith. First, faith in oneself – the faith to let the Ring go and for one to be restored to the lived-world with others, where there is no guarantee of absolute safety and power, but where there is also no doubt (or at least no *terminal, bottomless* doubt) about one's ability to negotiate this world – and faith in others, one's lived-world comrades – faith that they are not what our power-laden paranoid visions of threat would have us see in them, that they are not an unnavigable threat to our safety and security.

One cannot live without faith in (community with) others. Nor without faith in oneself. The Ring, through its promise of power and safety, seductively dangles before one a precious would-be harvest, namely the ability to do without these faiths; but reaping that harvest is reaping the whirlwind. It threatens implicitly simply to strip or to lacerate one of all faith, leaving one with nothing – or indeed with less than nothing. In this way, Frodo's psychic struggle can be played out outside his mind, and be grounded squarely in the world we share with others, in the way we navigate and manage this faithful living with others – mindful of the (personally and socially) devastating option of retreating from doing so – in politics.

The issue at the heart of *The Lord of the Rings* is then of almost *incalculable* importance, because it is the issue of the nexus of power, paranoia and terror which structures much of our contemporary political 'choices'. The nearest equivalent in our world to Sauron and his minions is George Bush's America (with Blair perhaps serving as Saruman). But the discourse of Bush and Blair themselves would, laughably but in *deadly* earnest, far easier see figures such as Bin Laden or Saddam Hussein as closer to Sauron than they themselves. This is the way in which paranoid thinking operates: it divides in Manichean fashion and it sees a minute threat as vast, the more it retreats from dealing with others in good faith as an equal would. The *more* powerful the USA becomes, and the more it retreats from the world, the *more* terrified it is of any threat. Thus in Reagan's dismal and pathetic 1980s America, for instance, Nicaragua seemed like a dagger pointing at the heart of Texas ...

The greatest task laid upon us by *The Lord of the Rings*, therefore, is not the pitiful, pointless and indeed hopeless effort (represented by Aragorn's coronation) to achieve a benevolent despotism (in the form, perhaps, of unchecked executive power in America, or of a public willingness to accept an utter abrogation of our individual liberties) into which we are tempted when we believe we are not safe, an effort that will surely only lead to sequels every bit as bloody (Afghanistan, Iraq ... Iran?) as the War of the Ring. No; the great task laid upon us by *The Lord of the Rings*, a task Tolkien himself seemingly failed to understand, is rather the effort, through the non-violent consciousness of Frodo, through the ecological consciousness of Treebeard, and through the empathetic social consciousness partially realized in Frodo and Bilbo and Gandalf and Aragorn – and fully realizable in Tolkien's/Jackson's audience, in you and me – to lay aside, or at least to come to terms with and not be dominated by, all that is represented in the Rings of Power; to accept the hard life of faith with ourselves and others.

*   *   *

Perhaps the most important injunction issued, then, is the one we probably want least, the most challenging one: we must try to understand the Sauron of our contemporary world. We must try to empathize with paranoid America. If we do not love it, it will fear more and more until it dominates and destroys the entire world, and then it will only 'learn' that its fears have been justified all along.

IV Art

Editor's Introduction

The short section that closes this book is two things:

1). a working through of what we take art to be, what we look for it to *do* in our lives; and (more generally)
2). an exercise in thinking differently.

The previous chapter, on *The Lord of the Rings*, links (from) politics (in)to art. It should be thought of as 'virtually' included in this section. But the essay below is very different from it. It is about art for art's sake, not for politics' sake.

It is an essay on aesthetics that challenges aesthetics – really to reach for the place it has etched out in current intellectual and lived discourse. We want art to be valued, perhaps above all else. We want it to be a vessel for human potential, a realization of brief meetings between mortals and something eternal. And, all at the same time, we want it to be … something …
else.

We want art to be grounded, to tell us something about our temporal, limited, ephemeral reality. We want to see ourselves reflected in it. We want it to be real and accessible and to play in the everyday. We want and expect art to have a message. We want it to be … something …
normal.

So the first function of this section's lone chapter (though, as suggested above, a reader would do well to figure Chapter 7 into the same discussion) is to explore this tension in art – the apparent contradiction in our expectation of it in our lives. It challenges aesthetics really to think through the demand 'art for art's sake', for when we do we are brought round to a different orientation for art in our lives, or our lives in art. We are asked to demand nothing of it other than for it to be art.

If this sounds like a puzzling conclusion, then you may see how the essay's second function is fundamentally embedded in its first. We are asked to entertain paradoxes – like the expectation for art to be real and super-real both at the same time – but *so as* ultimately to explode or dissolve or pass beyond them. This requires nothing short of thinking our way out of old modes of seeing and doing that are so familiar to us that we do not even realize or remember that they are there. This hard thinking is in many ways the conclusion to this book. And an action. In fact, it is both an action and a prerequisite for action. To think our way out of an apparent dead-end is to notice or understand that there are ways of moving forward that we fail to see …
and then to take them.

This recognition of what needs to be done, and how to do it, this last chapter shows, is art. It is also, however, what this entire book is about: it is philosophy; it is ethics; it is politics – and it is life.

8 Eliot for Art's Sake (or: The Ideal of an 'Actual Art')

'The novel's sole *raison d'etre* is to say what only the novel can say.' With these words, Milan Kundera[1] enunciates a powerful theory of the novel and, by extension, of art as a whole. A powerful precept for art-critical theory: that in each and every art form there has been (or should be) a gradual development over time towards making the most out of the possibilities inherent in that form and that form alone. Thus in film, for example, this process would mean a gradual movement towards exploiting film's unique moving visuals on/to the surface of the screen (combined with changing sounds too). Sequences of images and sounds which do not necessarily exploit illusions of depth or referentiality, but which simply *are*. Think of *avant-garde* animation, or indeed of portions of *Natural Born Killers*.

According to major art critic Clement Greenberg, this process in painting involved in the twentieth century an ever more pressing attention to the surface of the canvas, to emphasizing the nature of this surface and of the materials which are (on) it. This has been what abstraction, correlated with a steady move away from representationalism, has meant. But has this process gone as far as it can go towards the ideal outlined above? In other words: in the fine arts, is respected aesthetician Arthur Danto right to say that there is no more fundamental innovation to be achieved, that art history has come to an end; indeed, that it has been over for some time now?

Well, an *emphasis* on the surface of a painting still involves a kind of message; only the message has shifted *from* concerning something that the art represents and that is 'virtually' presented to us, *to* concerning the art's form, the Art-World, the possibilities of manipulating materials in various ways, and so on. But this then arguably falls short of the ideal of the drive towards a perfection of each art form; for the latter in fine art would surely involve surfaces and *objects as a whole* which simply were perfectly self-contained visually (and tactilely). If you like, images – but not images of – or about – anything; simply themselves, as something to see. (Or, in the case of literary art: words simply as something to be experienced.)

What artworks might satisfy this criterion? It would be art where – for the first time ever in art? – what you see is exactly what you actually see (and, perhaps, touch). It would be a kind of antithesis of 'conceptual art'. For while conceptual art is reducible to an idea, art as I am imagining it would not be reducible at all.

* * *

We will come shortly to how this can possibly be.

First, let us take a few moments to examine how exactly the sort of movement I have described in (perhaps somewhat complicated) brief above may have already come to fruition. Note that much of what (my paraphrasing of what) Danto says about modern art has often been said of Modernism *in general*. Thus, returning from Modernist visual to literary art forms[2] suggests that the truth, *contra* Danto, is that in Modernism (and modern art) the biggest illusion of all is invariably that the journey – history – is temporarily or permanently over. Just when you think that it is, then for that very reason something will turn up that shows that further change – in the present case innovation (and) approximation to an ideal of abstraction or of progress towards some goal internal to art, to the art form in question – has already begun. If it was ever right to say that art has ended, then here at the very least is an extension of that end into a new terrain.

Consider the case, in literature, of T. S. Eliot (who, recall, was once hailed as the paradigmatic Modernist). It seems, given what one gleans as the 'point' of his critical work, that he would have liked his poetry to be seen as communicating things that are ultimately in themselves (as opposed to in their mode of presentation) not much different from things that might be communicated in a set of theoretic assertions in a plodding philosopher's thesis. Eliot wanted his art to *say* things. In this insistence he seems to have failed to have understood just how fine his own grasp of the musicality and philosophically astute tonality of English – of poetry – could be when left *in* poetry, and thus of the (still) very new, and (at least at that time mostly unexplored) artistic value of poetry itself. In this way, Eliot's observation that 'The reader's interpretation [of a poem] may differ from the author's and be equally valid – it may even be better ...'[3] is poignantly correct when applied to his own work. For instance, I suspect that the very best 'interpretations' of the *Four Quartets* are mostly not those that Eliot himself offered. Reading as Eliot does, one may easily miss the extraordinary (and, I believe, important) *sound* of lines such as: 'Distracted from distraction by distraction,/Filled with fancies and empty of meaning ...'

Here, the plainness of 'empty of meaning' contrasts significantly with the qualitatively complex sound of the line-and-a-half preceding it.

One does not hear the word-music here deeply enough unless one pays specific attention to the way the rhythms and repetitions in the poem are *not separable* from the philosophizing on the nature of time, of meaning, and so on.

In his important essay *The Music of Poetry* [4] (1924), Eliot remarks: 'the poem means more, not less, than ordinary speech can communicate'. Yes; but I would claim that a deeply rewarding interpretation of the *Four Quartets* would pay *more* attention to the musicality of and the 'display' of language in that poem than Eliot in fact does. The sound of presented paradoxes and indeed of conceptual impossibilities,

impossibilities that force one to philosophize for oneself from them: that is what Eliot, I think, (almost unknowingly) gives us in the greatest passages in 'Burnt Norton' and 'Little Gidding' (and in the poem's 'coda') in particular. That is how a poem means 'more', not less, than 'ordinary language': simply by being what it is. It is not that a good poem concentrates a heavy dose of ordinary meaning into a small pill of words. It is that it sounds or displays the ordinary – or nonsensical violations of the ordinary – and thus gives us a marvellous illusion of managing to mean so much, when in the ordinary sense *it does not mean anything at all.*

Eliot's poetry is deep word-music: the sound of sense and the sound of nonsense.

What is regrettable is that Eliot himself has too unsubtle and unpoetic a notion of what it is for a poem to communicate and so does not recognize the real value of his modernity while valuing other aspects of it (e.g. it's 'groundedness' in tradition, etc.). A poem should above all communicate *itself.* In theory, Eliot believed this (there are famous witty episodes of his refusing in various ways asinine requests for him to explain his poetry to listeners), but in not understanding this in much of the actual practice of his literary theory and criticism, and perhaps also by failing to stay true to this thought at some key moments in *Four Quartets*, Eliot probably communicates his own works without (or at least 'before') understanding them ...

Eliot's poetry, 'even' in the *Four Quartets*, is, I submit, at its best when it is starkly 'untranslatable', unparaphrasable. The language of great poetry is the language of paradox; great poetry, in my opinion very like the greatest philosophy, starkly and bluntly resists being prosified, largely because it retains a condition of paradoxicality even when (intelligently) spoken of or criticized. *Eliot's writing is greater and stranger than even he knows.*

* * *

There is more here than simply saying that Modernism and the greatest Modernists might have missed the (a)venues opened up for (rather than actually reaching the 'end' of) art. What is here, too, is that the Modernist 'end' of art may begin by engaging us in a thinking through of our embedded expectations of what art is to give us. This may (also) be seen (better) in another great Modernist writer, Wallace Stevens, because the latter's (also clearly philosophical) poetry has consistently stronger styles and distinctivenesses than Eliot's. Stevens (as with the unparaphrasable 'prose' of Faulkner or Woolf) develops more of a 'language' of his own, a 'language' that can never be our language, never be a language in use.

I would argue that Stevens, like many other great Modernists (such as Eliot) takes us to 'the other side' of language and finds the 'place' then reached to contain not ineffable truths, or thoughts that can't be uttered, or an indescribable formless realm, or even visions or acts of imagination, but simply the words, the sounds, the fabulous, sensuous, delicious, sometimes hysterical, sometimes weird or mad or unpleasant delusions of sense that they produce, that they *are the creations of*.[5] Many of Stevens' greatest works – such as '13 Ways of Looking at a Blackbird' and 'Anecdote of the Jar' – are, in the end, mostly ('about') just language. The language, language 'out of use', which iconically 'represents' only itself and which seemingly 'gestures at' a nothing that presents itself as a something about which nothing can be said ...

Clearly, though, this sort of presentation does not stop – indeed, it has certainly begun (or at least been concomitant with the beginning of) – an intense scrutiny of what we have when 'all we have' is language that has (arguably) preoccupied much of subsequent (verbal and visual) art and (certainly) western philosophy for the last half-century.[6] Arguably, then, we can now proceed still further than the internal dynamic of art's drive towards abstraction alone would suggest. On the far end or side of the road towards abstraction is a new possibility of art being, if you like, *intensely real and concrete*. The thing to do with such art may, phenomenologically, be: nothing. The art is perhaps mostly not there to think or speak about. (And the use of art functionally – e.g. simply to prop up a wall – is not a treating of it as art.)

What would art be like which didn't (try to) have any message that was paraphrasable, not even any kind of emotional message, or message about art, or 'about itself', or about the materials out of which it was constructed, or about there being no message? Perhaps we are beginning to understand what becomes of asking this question. Namely: art that (simply) is, or (over time) simply becomes.

There is perhaps an undesirable implication in the name that I am toying with here for such art, 'Actual Art'; a false contrast with 'potential'. For the potential of pieces of (actual) art is, as will be made clear, precisely to the point. But nevertheless, 'Actual Art', paradoxical and perverse and almost redundant though it may be as an appellation, may be peculiarly apt for this school, if a school it would be. For this art, if I am right in my contentions above, is not about anything imaginary, virtual, or real. It's just art – (and) just things (in) themselves. Not *about* themselves, just (*by*) themselves. (To be just a little too Zen about it: it just is what it (actually) is.)

* * *

Now, it could be argued that the 'messages' or 'contents' of works of 'Actual Art' concern the materials out of which the works are constructed. Clearly one's attention is often drawn immediately *to* those materials, but this is not the same as those works being about their materials, as perhaps Pollock's paintings can in some instances be said to be about the medium of paint, its viscosity, etc. The real novelty of the art I am meaning to describe, or to imagine, does not lie here.

It could also be argued that what much 'actual' art

(consider for instance much 'Earth Art', or 'Environmental Art') is about is change, the passage of time.[7] And this is an interesting possibility, for it works against the traditional notion of a 'timeless' work of art. But again, there is a vital difference between the depiction or intimation of the passage of time (think of Monet or of Dali) and the exposing of something to time's passage. If these works of art that I have in mind were, as it were, saying to their viewer 'Look at how time's passing alters everything!', or 'You see, it's not decay, it's simply change', then, while somewhat novel and thought-provoking, they would not be revolutionary in the sense that I have been suggesting. They would not, that is, avoid the dogma of content, of there being a sense in which the art was portraying or 'saying' something.

Now, it might be argued that in doing as little as continuing the use of the word 'art' we buy not only into a certain artsiness, into 'the Art-World', but also into some interest in 'content'. But this may beg the question at issue, for perhaps this new art is linked only historically and categorically to preceding art. Perhaps there has been a kink in the evolution of art such that we can evade 'the dogma of content' while still discussing something(s) worth calling 'art objects'; or, better perhaps, 'art things'.

I would propose that the art I am talking about is not 'about' change or time or even 'about' the impact of these on the materials employed. Rather, we can at most find the passage of time *exposed* in these art-things.[8] Better, because less abstractly: the changes in these pieces are open to view, as they themselves are literally exposed to some elements. (There is arguably no such thing as literally *exposing* something to time's passing; it's rather an ongoing change-trace that we see.) We do not see works depicting or commenting on the transience of it all; we simply see each work as it is, and realize in most cases without any need for reflection that at other moments it will surely be different. Naturally, the more organic and motion-involving pieces tend to change at a much more rapid rate than the metallic pieces. (Some of the former perceptibly change somewhat even as one is looking at them.) Some pieces will in fact change in ways or at rates which are highly unpredictable to someone not knowing exactly how the piece was constructed, say. But all will change. And will still be able to be called by the same name and essentially left alone. Somewhat tautologically: the work is what it is when it leaves the artist's hands (even, in a certain sense, before, also); and at all subsequent moments. There is just no presupposition any longer that it will ideally (and, of course, impossibly) be the same at all those moments. The process (of change) is not viewable in its totality. These are Heraclitean art-things, as opposed to Platonic art-objects. Now there's a real change!

It makes sense to speak of restoring a Pollock, a Boccioni, a Henry Moore, a Frank Stella, a Richard Long, a Michael Graves, even a Warhol or a Duchamp. Why? One feels that there is a way that these are supposed to look, (and) to stay the same. The same is perhaps most obviously true of conceptual art as a school. Here, the art (object) itself is almost irrelevant to the message – the concept – which is (supposedly) at its core. Such that if a piece of conceptual art were damaged, it would simply be obvious that it ought to be repaired so that it could continue to express the same concept as before. By contrast, here, in the works I am wanting to speak of, ideally, we have actual (art) things, and so no concept(s) to speak of.

We can see clearly how little fine art to date can be said to have advanced beyond the idea of having some kind of (conceptual or otherwise) content when we consider in any depth this question of the apparent need to restore art, including the examples just mentioned. We have not advanced beyond the dogma of content and paraphrasability until we are beyond the desire to – and the point of – 'restoration'. (We might add that the reification of the over-commercialized art-object is also subject to some challenge by the notion that restoration is a dangerous irrelevancy, and by a closer tying of the price of the metamorphosing art-thing to its materials.)

Whether it be a Michelangelo or a Moore or a Warhol, as it changes with the passage of time its aesthetic content should also change (at least slightly, with new shades, shadows, and so on). But we don't allow it to. What would art be that did not need to be restored? Even that in a certain sense could not be restored in principle, for there would no longer be any pristine original state conceptually available to restore it to. But further, how does one have a content that is untendentiously immune to the passage of time?

Nietzsche once said that each and every one of us ought to 'Become who you are'. This need not be read as Aristotelian essentialism; it can be seen instead as inherently existentially paradoxical. No determinate prediction, no hidden organic essence, but yet a certain arrow into the future. Perhaps the same idea can be applied to art. That is to say, perhaps the least bad answer available to the questions just asked, the only timely (and timeless?) way is: not to have art with content, but rather to have art that becomes whatever at any moment it is. Or more simply: art that becomes whatever.

All art might become (like) 'actual art', if only we could stop worrying about how the Sistine Chapel or the Mona Lisa was supposed to look and just let it (as us) metamorphose. But, to date, we – mostly – cannot. Of course, there would be costs to such 'object-liberation'. And it might be argued that we should not pay these costs, that we should keep the Sistine Chapel as a piece in a different art game, an old-fashioned game of essences. But, though there may be costs, there are also benefits, such as, for example, a continual sense of the freshness not only of the art of the present but also of those very great predecessors.

On this particular criterion of a lack of need for restoration, even in principle, one might cite some 'Earthworks',[9] and some Earth Art,[10] some 'Arte Povera', some performance art (e.g. some non-reperformable stuff), some of John Cage's less dogmatic work and some other artists as yet not that well known, such as Melissa Kretschmer, Nathan Joseph and Yutaka Kobayashi – or when one looks at the latter's work, such as 'Dust Rising' or 'Running' or 'Work in Progress' – one may see the process in close quarters at an advanced and exciting stage. The process, that is, of change in the art; and the process of change in our understanding of what art is and can be. Towards an alternative ideal of and for art!

At the 'end' of every road is a new road, a new avenue; and this is a (new) venue for art, a new branch of art, though right now it might seem to be one beyond which further branches are unenvisageable. Of course this is so, for if the next stage could be clearly envisioned, it would be now rather than next, it would already obviously be starting to happen. As with the great Louis Armstrong remark, 'If I knew where jazz was going, I'd be there already'. Also, however, notice that this art interestingly challenges the scope of conceptual envisioning per se; for the concreteness of many of these pieces at present defies easy – or even any – description and classification. As with some jazz …

Actual art, as I have accounted it, may constitute a new end of art; perhaps we are fated to live in a time when art, like philosophy, will always be 'ending'. The name 'Actual Art' might be taken to imply a penetration to the heart of what art is; but if so, the 'is', and the 'art', should not be taken timelessly. Actual art will surely in its turn be overtaken by new branches – and new 'ends' – of art. Again – and thankfully – at this time we have no idea what these will be. But notice a key point that emerges from this section of the discussion: the ideal of an actual art is perhaps unique in being able to account for its own future waning. Actual art and its ideal will themselves surely change and fade. As this happens, there will be no cause for regret. And the only difference will be: the ideal will wane, but most of the pieces will, in the relevant sense, only change.

When Shunryu Suzuki was asked for a definition of Zen, he replied 'Everything changes'. An art has begun that is prepared to live with the deep truth of that short sentence.

For *now* what we have is such a thing as (the ideal of, and some instances of, an) actual art, and it's a good thing too. There is arguably not much to be said about the pieces I am writing about as artworks, beyond the kind of things already said here.

*　　*　　*

But this, if correct, is a triumph. The person interacting with this art, seeing it at some moments in its evolution and perhaps altering it slightly, cannot usefully look for a – for any – content to or in it; this is something new. One – they – we – can and have to let the art be and become.

Some of this 'actual' art is perhaps ugly, much is surely beautiful, and much is really neither one nor the other. (Perhaps in this respect, like the best of Remedios Varos and Kandinsky and Rauschenberg and Stella and Cage, it just impresses us aesthetically without our being able to say much about why; one has to know when to stop, when to stop talking about art. This art mostly helps stifle this urge to talk, reasonably rapidly.)

Because, to sum up: a work of (actual) art just is whatever it is, and becomes whatever it actually becomes, over the course of its lifetime. In the words of Ludwig Wittgenstein: 'It is there – like our life'.[11] The ideal that I find in this 'actual art' is for each work simply to be (what it is) at each and any moment of its existence, not to have any kind of 'message' or 'content', but rather simply (to) change. Being in time.

When the medium is the message, then it still makes sense to talk of media and messages. Actual art is art of which it no longer makes sense even to talk of its being a medium (for messages of any kind). And without content, we might even venture that many of these art-things have no form at all, either (but rather *only* a shape, and a place). That governing dichotomy – of form and content – is finally, tardily, left behind. For it only makes sense to talk of form if and where it makes sense to talk of content.

Enough. Insofar as there is anything to be said about this art, perhaps it is the kind of thing I have said (and in fact severally repeated, in a spiralling effort to arrive at the correct formulation of an elusive newness). And the tension between the 'actualist' ideal I have laid out, on the one hand, and the aspects of these pieces which perhaps remain interpretable more along the lines of traditional representational and abstract art, on the other, is what makes for the individuality of each piece. That, and the sheer physico-temporal differences between them. But the key is that the latter is something that one needs only to experience, not to discuss.

That is why I have said almost nothing at all about the (extraordinary) specificity of works that I would consider 'actual art'. They are there, queerly self-sufficient, nothing more or less than their becoming(s). That is all.[12]

Conclusion: Philosophy for Life

This first decade of the third millennium is a time of vast peril and vast opportunity for humankind. The perils include:

- the possible drowning of art in and by commercialism and 'entertainment';
- the atomization of human beings by economic neo-liberalism such that ethical and political action and politically engaged spirituality is sidelined and only aggressive evangelical fundamentalism is left to confront liberalism in a mutually poisonous embrace;
- consumerism taking a deeper hold such that 'choice' is all that seems to matter and real rights and wrongs are taken instead to be 'optional';
- increased market-based exploitation of and suffering in the non-human world;
- PR and 'spin' taking a stronger hold of our public discourse such that the very language that we need in order to understand and resist what is going on is deformed;
- a loss of the vocabulary of true virtue, forgiveness, etc., in favour of a self-centred vocabulary of achieving would-be psychological calm, no matter what the cost;
- a vicious circle of repressive laws and paranoid security apparatuses that produce violent or conspiratorial responses that seem to 'prove' that yet more repression is needed;
- uncontrolled materialism and continued 'economic growth';
- climate chaos;
- climate catastrophe.

In this huge setting, the forces of philosophy may seem paltry. How can philosophy possibly 'come to the rescue'? At any rate, if all it has to offer is the power of the critical human intellect, compared with the power of the dollar and the bomb and the ultimate weapon of mass destruction, catastrophic climate change.

But I have tried to suggest that there *is* a real role for philosophy hereabouts. Partly because it need *not* be thought of as narrowly as it usually is, as rational theory building and purely intellectual reflection. It can instead be thought of as a returning afresh and being more self-aware of what we already know – as always-already-applied, as part of a 'therapy' for self and society that treats our illnesses – and offers the outline of something beyond them. Philosophy can be a radical and powerful tool for starting something good.

In Section I of this book, I urged that we remind ourselves of our embeddedness in the ecosystem (Chapter 1). And (Chapter 2) that we take seriously the challenge of climate chaos (not 'climate change' – that's far too anodyne a term with which to index this most cataclysmic threat of all) and think beyond market-mania towards new ideas on which to base our society (including revitalizing *old* ideas, such as rationing).

I suggested, in sum, that philosophical reflection on our *environment* (better, on *ecology*) must at this point in history increase the importance for us of this concept. Or rather, of the reality which will force us to recognize the importance of it, if we do not get there first ...

In Section II, I counselled that what is needed at this point in history to engage our psychological and our spiritual needs is 'politically engaged' spirituality. But that means that religion must be allowed to be a practice and not just confined to private domains (Chapter 3). But nor must deep religious and ethical impulses be *subjugated* to politics (see Chapters 3 and 5); true religion/spirituality – what I like to call 'consciousnessality' – *comes* from within and *acts* without (Chapters 3 and 4). I also suggested that there are limits to what philosophy can hope to contribute to sorting out some of the questions that most vex us in this area, such as what we ought or ought not to fear most and how it is possible to forgive (Chapter 5). I urged a certain humility in the face of the wonder and horror of human life. I urged that, to coin a Quaker term, we do not stop being humble 'seekers' after truth, rather than imagining that we are already finders.

In Section III, I went further into the 'reclamation' of our language begun in Section I. I suggested that we cannot reclaim politics unless we reclaim the English language, and I suggested that in this regard Wittgenstein, Chomsky and Orwell all point in the same direction (Chapter 6). I urged the value (in Chapter 7) of great mythic trilogies such as Tolkien's *The Lord of the Rings*, Pullman's *Dark Materials* and Nix's *Old Kingdom* trilogy in returning us to political wisdom. Works such as these re-teach us the psychological, psychopathological and quasi-religious roots of political power, its promises and its pathologies.

Finally, in Section IV, I moved from thinking of art for politics' sake to thinking of art for art's sake. The world I would like to see emerge in the twenty-first century is one in which we can afford the luxury of the splendid self-exposing art that was the greatest product, in my view, of Modernism. The kind of word-musical, self-subsistent, linguistic-philosophical poetry written by Eliot or Stevens – and the kind of becoming-art, changing-art that is created by artists willing to let their art *be*, and even by the Earth itself – these, to me, are 'actual art' (Chapter 8).

It would be a fine thing if art and religiosity could exist more for their own sake than for the sake of politics or of survival. In order to make that one day possible, I submit that first we will have to get our political (including vitally, of course, our ecological) house in order. And philosophy has a role here. Philosophy now has to be ethical and political. And that is what much of this book has been (about).

The natural reading of 'Philosophy for Life' is: philosophy for *life* ... philosophy for our actual lives, not just for a fantasy of those lives; philosophy for more or less everyday dilemmas and edification, not just philosophy for a sterile study or a claustrophobic classroom.

But I mean the book's title in another way, too: Philosophy *for* Life ... That is, philosophy *on the side of* life. The fundamental question of the twenty-first century is whether human life as we know it, human civilization, will survive at all. As sketched above, there are various ways that it could quite possibly perish as a result of state or non-state war/terrorism. More likely still, runaway climate change could wreck it more completely than any bomb.

Philosophy has something to offer in this struggle, the struggle of humankind to attain a better existence and (first and foremost) to retain an existence, *because* it can be more than just the (wonderful) critical self-reflection of the human spirit. It can be intrinsically applied. It can be an organic *part* of the ethical struggle to save the humans.

Philosophy is the love of wisdom. Beloved wisdom ought always to be on the side of life against the forces of self-destructiveness that right now have such a grip on our economies, our polities, our psyches. When one says, as I have said in this book, that we have to see ourselves as inextricably part of a fragile ecosystem, then that is philosophy, *and* that is a selves-seeing that will inexorably impact on how one acts. If one acts in such a way that is compatible with what one sees and what one thinks, one will act well. Out of faith (in us, in life, in 'applied consciousness'). Out of hope ... We must dare to hope. It is so tempting to give up hope, but to do so creates a self-fulfilling prophecy. The great temptation to feel safe through placing oneself, actually or psychologically, in a position where there is nothing to hope for or trust in is a great delusion. To retain hope, and trust, is a necessity that never stops. Let us all dare never to give up hoping, never to stop trying, never to lose the faith.

The twenty-first century is a time of vast opportunity for

humankind. We (in the West) are wallowing in riches; we have material abundance, enough to share with all. Our technological abilities are enormous; we have magnificent cultural wealth and, while *economic* globalization has mostly been a political and human disaster, the spread of global *communications* has created many wonderful human possibilities to share wisdom that did not exist as recently as a generation ago. As I have intimated above, we could build a peaceful civilization in which art and consciousness flourish. We could build a green utopia. We could have a philosophy, a politics, a life, that is *for life*.

So now: the rest is up to you. The next steps are up to you. Or rather, to all of us together. We will sink or swim together. It is up to you as well as to me to ensure that philosophy is for life: in the water, in the air and on the land of this glorious and astonishing Earth. For always.

Further Reading

The suggested further reading listed here is of course in addition to the texts discussed in the body of the chapters above. It is worth remarking that the suggestions for further reading below all more or less overlap, spilling across the sectional divides that my editor and I used to try to impose order on this book. There is I think a lesson here, concerning the holistic nature of the issues discussed in the book. Perhaps the reader shares a growing sense of this book, which perhaps appeared initially to be about a whole lot of different things, as something of a unified whole after all ... See also http://rupertread.fastmail. co.uk and http://www.uea.ac.uk/~j339/ for versions of my essays available online.

Environment

The Green Economics Institute website is a reasonably good place to start: http://www.greeneconomics.org.uk/

The leading green/ecological economist is Herman Daly. His work is extremely philosophically stimulating; it is, simply, vital. I recommend, for instance, his *Beyond Growth* (Boston, MA: Beacon, 1996). For a slightly more empirically based discussion, read Richard Douthwaite's splendid and deeply concerning book, *The Growth Illusion* (Totnes: Green Books, 1999). For a more psychologically based approach, Clive Hamilton's work is excellent: read his *Affluenza* (London: Allen and Unwin, 2006) or his *Growth Fetish* (London: Pluto, 2004). The much maligned *Limits to Growth* (London: EarthScan, 2005), by Donella Meadows, Jorgen Randers and Dennis Meadows is unfortunately being proved more right with each passing day. Read it to understand why.

Joel Kovel's philosophical masterpiece of eco-socialism, *The Enemy of Nature: The End of Capitalism or the End of the World?* (London: Zed Books, 2002), is not to be missed. To understand how carbon rationing will work, read Mayer Hillman's powerful *How We Can Save the Planet* (London: Penguin, 2004). (Mayer once confided to me that he regretted not entitling it *How We Must Save the Planet*. Yes indeed.)

For a work that begins by critiquing the philosophy of economics of Adam Smith *et al,* and ends with a *set* of extremely practicable eco-friendly policy recommendations, look no further than Mike Woodin and Caroline Lucas's *Green Alternatives to Globalization: A Manifesto* (London: Pluto, 2004).

My essay 'Contract liberalism cannot take future generations seriously' – available online at http://rupertread.fastmail. co.uk/ Future%20generations.doc – details my own philosophical account of the way that environmental concerns must henceforth inform political philosophy.

Religion

For a superb philosophical 'deconstruction' of supernaturalistic monotheism, one should read Plato's *Euthyphro* online at: http://etext.library.adelaide.edu.au/mirror/classics.mit.edu/ Plato/euthyfro.html. The spiritual roots of consumerism and the path to a practical spirituality of love are beautifully set out in the work of Erich Fromm. See especially his *To Have or to Be?* (London: Jonathan Cape, 1978).

For a book that draws together the lessons of contemplative religion in a way that responds precisely to the current condition of the world, I *highly* recommend Eckhart Tolle's remarkable new book, *A New Earth* (London: Penguin, 2005).

To understand (and practice?) Buddhism as a westerner, there can be no better guide than Shunryu Suzuki, whose (too few) books are all entirely apposite and magical. As a primer for engaged spirituality, David Brazier's *The New Buddhism* (London: Robinson, 2001) is perhaps the best place to start; Ken Jones's work is also very well worth reading.

Wittgenstein's *Lectures and Conversations on Aesthetics, Psychology and Religious Belief* (edited by Cyril Barrett; Berkeley: University of California Press, 1972), especially the opening pages of the 'Lectures on Religious Belief', is a very powerful pointer away from and beyond crudely literal or supernaturalistic interpretations of religion and towards something much more attractive.

Politics

The British Noam Chomsky is Mark Curtis. If you haven't read him, then start with his *Web of Deceit: Britain's Real Role in the World* (London: Vintage, 2003). For the original Orwell essay that has inspired Chomsky and Curtis and a number of other philosophers, go to http://www.mtholyoke.edu/acad/intrel/orwell46.htm.

Philosophical cognitive linguist George Lakoff has become a compelling figure to read on how best to 'reframe' political issues. His books are fascinating, important and deeply useful; go to http://www.rockridgeinstitute.org/, http://www.rockridgeinstitute.org/people/lakoff, or http://www.georgelakoff.com/ to get started.

For the best extant criticism of the 'political liberalism' that rules contemporary political philosophy, read anything that you find accessible by Alasdair MacIntyre. If you liked my psycho-political interpretation of *The Lord of the Rings*, you might want more: see my essay 'The fantasy of safety through power: the psycho-political philosophy of *The Lord of the Rings*' at http://www.uea.ac.uk/~j339/LOTR2.htm.

For a realizable vision of a better political future, a full political philosophy for the twenty-first century, see my (forthcoming) book, *The Green Manifesto*, joint-authored with Phil Hutchinson.

Art

Eliot's *Four Quartets* is compulsory reading for anyone interested in a 'philosophical' poetry: go to http://www.tristan. icom43.net/quartets/. Some of Wallace Stevens' greatest and most philosophically fascinating poetry is collected at http:// www.writing.upenn.edu/~afilreis/88/stevens-poems.html.

James Guetti's *Wittgenstein and the Grammar of Literary Experience* (Athens, GA: University of Georgia Press, 1993) is in my opinion the most stimulating literary-critical work drawing on philosophy that has ever been written. It is itself a kind of work of art.

And lastly, if you want to go deeper into the thinking of Wittgenstein, the greatest philosopher of modern times whose work underlies key moments in all four sections of this book, then the best place to start is probably Ray Monk's very readable philosophical biography, *Ludwig Wittgenstein: The Duty of Genius* (New York: Free Press, 1990). In fact, perhaps a suitable 'retrospective epigraph' can be found in a letter from Wittgenstein quoted by Monk on p. 324: 'It is all the same to me what the professional philosophers of today think [...]; for it is not for them that I am writing.'

Notes

Editor's Introduction

1. This definition is taken from the web page of the Society for Applied Philosophy – http://www.appliedphil.org – which oversees Blackwell's *Journal of Applied Philosophy* out of the University of London's School of Advanced Study, and which might be considered the international authority on applied philosophy.
2. Ludwig Wittgenstein, 'Lecture on Ethics', J. Klagge and A. Nordmann (eds), *Philosophical Occasions* (Indianapolis, IN: Hackett, 1993), p. 44.
3. There are, of course, 'desert island' scenarios which may seem, at first, to challenge this claim, but really all they do is to highlight the deep connection we have with ethics, how unshakable, ultimately, such living is; think of *Robinson Crusoe* or (possibly) *The Lord of the Flies*, or such films as *Apocalypse Now* and *Castaway*.
4. See not only Wittgenstein's work, but also Kierkegaard's, Nietzsche's and Socrates's. For more discussion, see Alexander Nehamas's *The Art of Living* (Berkeley: University of California Press, 1998).

I Environment

1 We Are Part of Our Ecosystem

1. I employ this term in Cornel West's affirmative sense; *vida The American Evasion of Philosophy: A Genealogy of Pragmatism* (Madison, WI: University of Wisconsin Press, 1989), p. 36, and pp. 87–96, *et passim*.

2. See such a defence, perhaps the most theoretically compelling, in Paul Taylor's *Respect for Nature: A Theory of Environmental Ethics* (Princeton, NJ: Princeton University Press, 1986); *vida* pp. 80–118 for his problematic use of the term 'Nature'.

3. Effectually argued in Patrick Murphy's (1988) 'Sex-typing the planet: Gaia imagery and the problem of subverting Patriarchy', *Environmental Ethics* 10: 2, pp. 155–168.

4. Consult his *Logic: The Theory of Inquiry* (New York: Holt, Rinehart, Winston, 1938), *A Common Faith* (New Haven, CT: Yale Press, 1934), *Experience and Nature* (La Salle, IL: Open Court, 1925), and *Democracy and Education* (Toronto: Collier-MacMillan, 1916; particularly the first four chapters). Throughout the *Logic* in particular, Dewey emphasizes both the continuity of inquiry with (other) organic behaviour, and the 'profound interpenetration' of the 'physical' and the 'cultural', which leads naturally to the conclusion that both are artificial idealizations.

5. Compare Chapter 3, below.

6. Dewey, *A Common Faith*, p. 53.

7. Elizabeth Harlow (1992), 'The Human Face of Nature' *Environmental Ethics* 14: 1, pp. 27–42; C. Manes (1988), 'Philosophy and the Environmental Task', *Environmental Ethics* 10: 1: 28, pp. 75–82.

8. Harlow, 29.

9. One might say rather (being more strictly Wittgensteinian): there is no word that does not have a perfectly fine everyday use(s), but we can't metaphysically 'lean on' words (for example, on *culture* and *nature*). We go astray when we take these words to mean something 'deep'.

10. It is of course vital that some truly wild places are kept in the world. But at least in all those places where the human hand has already made quite a difference, it would be very odd to insist that human technology should not ever be used to rescue or 'improve' them.

11. The key design method for achieving this goal (of 'permanent' human culture) is 'permaculture': i.e. constructing systems for human living whereby *there is no waste*, but rather the systems are more or less stable ecosystems in which every creature and product gets fed back into the system.

2 The Cost of Growth: Climate Change, Crisis and Chaos

1. Andrew Revkin, 'Saving the world and ourselves,' *The Sunday Telegraph, The New York Times Supplement,* 5 November 2006, p. 1.
2. As reported, for example, in Oliver Tickell's 'Wave, wind, sun and tide is a powerful mix', *Guardian,* 12 May 2005.
3. Visit them at www.gci.org.uk.
4. The best of which, by the way, do NOT run on industrial-scale biofuels: see Boswell's 'The new climate change cynicism', 25 March 2006, at www.oneworldcolumn.org/99.html.
5. Flight Pledge Union at www.flightpledge.org.uk.
6. The *White Paper on the Ethical Dimensions of Climate Change* (University Park, PA: Rock Ethics Institute) by Brown *et al* (2005) is an encouraging step in the right direction.
7. Many thanks to M. A. Lavery for his efforts in compiling and making cohesive much of the content of this chapter.

II Religion

3 Religion Without Belief: The Example of Quakerism's Political 'Consequences'

1. Grateful acknowledgments to M. A. Lavery, Steve Davison, Anne De Vivo, Phil Hutchinson and John Sisko for inspiration and constructive criticism on portions of this essay.
2. Ludwig Wittgenstein (1978), *Culture and Value* (Chicago, IL: University of Chicago Press), p. 28e.
3. Tony Judt, 'Bush's useful idiots', *London Review of Books,* 21 September 2006, p. 5.
4. The term 'liberal' here is used by me in a very broad sense: not only 'Liberals' but social democrats and moderate conservatives are in this sense 'liberals'. The alternative to liberalism is radicalism of various kinds: where a 'radical' is someone who believes that a particular 'comprehensive' conception of the good life can and should be legislated for by the state. A 'Liberal' is someone who

believes that the state can and should remain neutral between different 'comprehensive' conceptions of the good.

5. See, for example, pp. xxi ff. of his *Political Liberalism* (New York: Columbia University Press, 1993). See also p. xl, for the spelling out of how such 'neutrality' is understood, in the later Rawls.

6. From his *Collected Papers* (Harvard, MA: Harvard University Press, 1999), p. 611 (emphasis added).

7. *Political Liberalism, op. cit.,* p. xii.

8. See his (1999), *op, cit.,* pp. 449–72.

9. In other words, I envision my non-liberal (yet deeply pro-most-civil-liberties) vision being achievable through a re-localization of the world through its being the basis of interdependent yet semi-autonomous *communities* of faith and practice.

10. Greg Pahl – in 'Christocentric and Universalist Friends: Moving beyond the Stereotypes' – and Marty Grundy – in 'In the Presence of God' – have cast some interesting light obliquely on these questions, in the pages of *Friends Journal* (41:1, 1995). In compelling interlocking pieces, they have shown how deep differences in the nature of beliefs or faiths can be rendered moot by means of an emphasis on the commonality of many of our experiences and spiritual practice and a genuine sharing on the basis of equal respect.

11. One thinks here of 1). how clearly discernible prayers or hymns when uttered 'with feeling' are from these things as *merely* said, and 2). how rare it is to come across such felt utterances in a host of religious ceremonies which are often *obviously* only traditional markers of secular life 'achievements'. This is not to say that undertaking religious rituals in this way is necessarily meaningless or empty, only that there are times when 'religious' utterances (think here: 'Oh my god!') or religious ceremonies can be performed out of something other than personal conviction.

12. But not all. Keep in mind that I am giving in this section only *one* example. Much of what I say can at least to some degree be cross-applied to other religions like Buddhism, Taoism and Islamic Sufism (insofar *as these can be called 'religions' at all*). In fact, arguably *all* religions have a similarly contemplative wing.

What is special about Quakerism is that the whole is such a wing: like Buddhism, it is *predominantly* contemplative. (I am a Buddhist Quaker, incidentally ...)

13. To those who know Quakerism, it will be clear that I am primarily discussing here 'unprogrammed' Quaker meetings, not the quasi-evangelical Quakerism of the American West and of parts of Africa.

14. Thomas Kuhn, *The Structure of Scientific Revolutions* (Chicago, IL: University of Chicago Press, 1962).

15. On which, see Tom Young (1995), '"A project to be realized": global liberalism in contemporary Africa', *Millenium: Journal of International Studies* 24: 3: 527–46.

4 Which is Worse: Death or Dying?

1. As Wittgenstein famously held, death is not an *event in* life. With death, life does not change, or go through some special state. It simply ends. See, below p. 61.

2. Ludwig Wittgenstein, *Tractatus Logico-Philosophicus* (London: Kegan Paul, 1922), § 6.4311.

3. Martin Heidegger, *Being and Time* (New York: HarperCollins, 1962). See particularly Division Two, Chapter 1.

4. For discussion, see Jerry Goodenough's introduction to Read and Goodenough, *Film as Philosophy* (London: Palgrave, 2005).

5. One thinks here of the great Christian Aid slogan, 'We believe in life before death'.

6. This is the sense in which some existentialists like Albert Camus (see particularly his *The Myth of Sisyphus and Other Essays* (New York: Vintage International, 1991)) believe that existence, understood in its paramountcy as consciousness of one's existence, trumps even perpetual torment: 'It is during [the return of Sisyphus' rock from near the summit of a mountain to the top of which he has been condemned forever to roll it], that pause, that Sisyphus interests me ... That hour, like a breathing-space which returns as surely as his suffering, that is the hour of

consciousness. At each of these moments when he leaves the heights and gradually sinks toward the lairs of the gods, he is superior to his fate. He is stronger than his rock'. (p. 119)

7. Thanks for comments on and suggestions about this essay to Chrys Gitsoulis and (most heartily) M. A. Lavery.

5 (How) Is Forgiveness Possible?

1. Needless to say, on many occasions this cannot be done, such as on most occasions when someone wants to say something 'metaphysical'. See, for instance, the closing paragraphs of Wittgenstein's *Tractatus Logico-Philosophicus* (London: Kegan Paul, 1922).

2. I have in mind, for example, the position of some of those whom one encounters in Ron Rosenbaum's *Explaining Hitler* (London: Macmillan, 1998), who argue that we must not allow our greater understanding of Hitler to lessen our condemnation of him. An even more interesting position is that the very attempt to understand or explain Hitler is *itself* obscene.

3. 'Supernaturalistic explanations' are modelled on scientific explanations and mirror all the latter's flaws. To say that forgiveness happens because of the miraculous intervention of angels or spirits, for example, is no better – no more helpful to us in getting some where in understanding the very possibility of forgiving – than it would be to say it happens because some people have a 'forgiveness gene'.

4. These are my words, my paraphrase; for Derrida's words, and for detail, see his 'The Time of the King', *Given Time: I: Counterfeit Money* (Chicago, IL: University of Chicago Press, 1992) and also p. 40f. of *The Gift of Death* (Chicago, IL: University of Chicago Press, 1995).

5. Here, we might note the words of Antjie Krog, from p. 109 of her powerful account of the TRC, *The Country of my Skull* (London: Jonathan Cape, 1998): 'Once, there were two boys, Tom and Bernard. Tom lived right opposite Bernard. One day, Tom stole

Bernard's bicycle and everyday Bernard saw Tom cycling to school on it. After a year, Tom went up to Bernard, stretched out his hand and said, "Let's reconcile and put the past behind us."// Bernard looked at Tom's hand. "And what about the bicycle?"// "No," said Tom, "I'm not talking about the bicycle – I'm talking about reconciliation".'

6. TRC, Public Discussion, 12 March, 1998; quoted in Rosemary Jolly's 'South Africa's Truth and Reconciliation Commission: Modernity and their Discontents', *American Philosophical Association* 98:2, 1995: 109–15. See also sections 4 and 5 of Mamdani's 'Reconcilliation without Justice', in *Religion and Media* (Stanford, CA: University of Stanford Press, 2001).

III Politics

6 How I Learned to Love Noam Chomsky

1. Ludwig Wittgenstein, *Philosophical Investigations* (London: Blackwell, 2001), § 116.
2. Of course, Chomsky's 'first' reputation is as a celebrated linguist at MIT. I am as suspicious at his theorizing and language use in this area as I am willing to praise his clarity in issues political. See my 'How I learned to love (and hate) Noam Chomsky', in *Philosophical Writings* 15 & 16, 2000/1: 23–48.
3. See, for example, his *Radical Priorities* (Montreal: Black Rose, 1981).
4. Noam Chomsky, *Deterring Democracy* (New York: Hill and Wang, 1991), pp. 109–110.
5. For powerful ongoing analysis of the 'mainstream' corporate media's routine distortion of these matters, see www.medialens.org
6. *Op. cit.*, p. 119.
7. Ibid., p. 121.
8. Noam Chomsky, *What Uncle Sam Really Wants* (Berkeley, CA: Odonian Press, 1991), pp. 86–91.
9. The next chapter takes up this discussion in an interesting way.

10. An aside here given an invocation of Hitler: It is interesting to note how precisely this sort of talk – the ahistorical, decontextualized attribution of rightness (say as of saving the world from a dictator, a Hitler) and particularly the invocation of a *legacy* of rightness – helps those currently in power to justify present-day atrocities and illegalities. In the run-up to the attack on Iraq in 2002–3, just as in 1990–1, we were often told that Saddam was 'a new Hitler'. This was silly propaganda: Hitler led the most powerful armed forces in the world, whereas Saddam's army was only a pitiful remnant. But invoking the ghost of the Second World War seemed to help Blair and Bush 'justify' their illegal war of aggression.

11. Many thanks to Juan Cole for inspiring this comparison (and therefore much of what follows).

7 Rings, *Power, Fear and Politics*

1. (Much of) this material will soon be republished in a complete volume on the philosophical and (perhaps most importantly) psychological considerations raised by *The Lord of the Rings*.

2. And Philip Pullman …

3. As we shall see, the truth comes to be less that one possesses such power (the Ring) than that one is *possessed by* it. And here it is of no small interest to my argument that one is said to be (e.g.) 'a man *possessed*', if one is 'mad'.

4. The refuge is temporary only. Is this because any search for a permanent or at least indefinitely temporally infallible state or place of refuge is self-defeating, for reasons long understood by meditators and mystics? I submit that *The Lord of the Rings* is onto this deep spiritual truth, and tends indeed to extend one's understanding of it: one must not go to meditation to escape, or for safety. If one does, one's fears may be effectively repressed, but will then return, worse than before. *One must instead use a method of bare attention*, or some similar method. One must be ready and willing to sit with all that (one) is. True meditation is

not a refuge; it is in fact a particular and indeed intense kind of attention to the world, (and) to 'oneself'. One must not enter into meditation with the *aim* of achieving some inner peace, for instance.

5. I am thinking here of, at least, my own efforts to challenge the metaphors of 'different world', etc. – see my 'On Interpreting Schizophrenia via Wittgenstein', *Philosophical Psychology* 14(4), 2001 – especially the discussion of Kuhn's doctrine of 'one-and-a half' worlds, on p. 179 – in mine and Sharrock's *Kuhn* (Cambridge: Polity, 2002). Such a challenge implicitly informs my argument that the 'world' one then finds is only ever so in *scare*-quotes.

6. In Aragorn's words to Frodo: 'They are neither living nor dead … They will never stop hunting you'. See Jackson's (2001) *The Fellowship of the Ring* (USA: New Line Cinema).

7. This is an obvious point at which to bring in Buddhism to dissolve the problematics of *The Lord of the Rings*. One might start by comparing the Nazgul to Buddhism's 'hungry ghosts'.

8. This is not quite true; there is one that we do see – the Ring's elixir-like power to prolong life. This quasi-Dorian-Gray-ish power is notably of a piece with the way in which the Ring gives one dominion in a (private) 'world'. The Ring tantalizingly offers one a kind of seeming immortality. In the persons of the Ring-wraiths, of course, we see what such 'immortality' may actually mean. In other words: the power of the Ring to prolong life is not in the end a positive power at all. It is a disastrous temptation, a gradually looming loss of self, a road to wraithdom.

9. Recall, this is just after Frodo's desperately sad and empty speech to Sam on the slopes of Mount Doom: 'I can't remember the taste of fruit, nor the sound of water, nor the touch of grass. Naked and dark. There's nothing. No veil between me and the wheel of fire. I can see Him … with my waking eyes!' The nightmare is present in the daytime. See Jackson's (2003) *The Return of the King* (USA: New Line Cinema).

IV Art

8 Eliot for Art's Sake (or: The ideal of an 'Actual Art')

1. *The Art of the Novel* (New York: Harper Collins, 1989), p. 5.
2. These 'technical' terms obscure an important similarity between 'literary' and 'visual' art that is, I hope, about to be made clear, namely: literature is no *less* visual than painting, sculpture, etc. – particularly when that literature is highly imagistic (in such cases it could be thought of as twice visual – one sees the words and then pictures what they describe (if one, in fact, can)).
3. Quoted in R. J. McMaster's Fire and Ice (Don Mills, Ont., Canada: Longman, 1970).
4. (Glasgow: Jackson, Son, & Co., 1942), p. 2.
5. For more on this with particular reference to the (roughly parallel) case of Faulkner, see my (2003) 'Literature as Philosophy of Psychopathology: William Faulkner as Wittgensteinian', Philosophy, Psychiatry and Psychology 10: 2, pp. 115–24.
6. Perhaps the best example of this is Wittgenstein's masterpiece: *Philosophical Investigations* (London: Blackwell, 2001).
7. By this point it should be clear that we have transitioned back into a discussion of visual art exclusively. Much literary art cannot be properly understood to make such a statement as it is not subject to any change from the passage of time (i.e. while a certain print-maker's work can fade, it would be odd to say that, for instance, Shakespeare's language 'fades'; certainly it can be translated into contemporary diction, etc., but the 'actualness' of the words themselves is immaterial and thus not subject to change conceived as it is in the text, *supra*).
8. C.f. the previous note on translating Shakespeare's language into contemporary diction. In this sense, the difference between visual and verbal art is diminished, as I believe should be the result of adopting an 'Actual Art' view of art.
9. Compare, for example, Long from the year 2000, and some of the work of Andy Goldsworthy.
10. Type 'Earth Art' into Google, to see some of what I mean.

11. Ludwig Wittgenstein, *On Certainty* (Oxford: Blackwell, 1969),
§ 559.

12. Many thanks are due to Anne De Vivo, Aaron Meskin, and Doug
Sobers for discussion and comments. Also, thanks to all those
who worked at and directed the former Fulcrum Gallery SoHo,
NYC, where the explicit idea of Actual Art was born.

Bibliography

Batchelor, S. (1997), *Buddhism Without Beliefs: A Contemporary Guide to Awakening*. London: Riverhead.

Booth, A. and Jacobs, H. (1990), 'Ties that bind: Native American Beliefs as a Foundation for Environmental Consciousness'. *Environmental Ethics* 12(1): pp. 27–43.

Boswell, A., 'The New Climate Change Cynicism', 25 March 2006, retrieved 12 November 2006 from http://www.oneworldcolumn.org/99.html.

Brazier, D. (2001), *The New Buddhism*. London: Robinson.

Brown, D., Tuana, N., Averill, M., Baer, P., Born, R., Brandão, C. E. L., Campos, C. P., Frodeman, R. Hogenhuis, C., Heyd, T., Lemons, J., McKinstry, R., Lutes, M., Miguez, J. D. G., Müller, B., Munasinghe, M., de Araujo, M. S. M., Nobre, C., Ott, K., Paavola, J., Rosa, L.P., Rosales, J., Rose, A., Wells, E., and Westra, L. (2005), *White Paper on the Ethical Dimensions of Climate Change*. University Park, PA: Rock Ethics Institute. Retrieved 12 November 2006 from http://rockethics.psu.edu/climate/whitepaper-intro.htm.

Camus, A. (1991), *The Myth of Sisyphus and Other Essays*. New York: Vintage International.

Chomsky, N. (1991), *Deterring Democracy*. New York: Hill and Wang.

— (1991), *What Uncle Sam Really Wants*. Berkeley, CA: Odonian Press.

— (1981), *Radical Priorities*. Otero, C. (ed), Montreal: Black Rose.

Christian Aid. 'The Climate of Poverty: Facts Fears and Hope', *In Depth*. Retrieved 12 November 2006 from http://www.christian-aid.org.uk/indepth/605caweek/index.htm.

Collard, A. and Contrucci, J. (1989), *Rape of the Wild: Man's Violence against Animals and the Earth*. Bloomington, IN: Indiana University Press.

Crary, A. and Read, R. (eds) (2000), *The New Wittgenstein*. London: Routledge.

Curtis, M. (2003), *Web of Deceit: Britain's Real Role in the World*. London: Vintage.

Daly, H. (1996), *Beyond Growth*. Boston: Beacon.

Daly, M. (1984), *Pure Lust*. London: The Women's Press Ltd.

Defoe, D. (1925), *Robinson Crusoe*. Philadelphia: The John C. Winston Company.

Derrida, J. (1995), *The Gift of Death*. Chicago: University of Chicago Press.

— (1992), 'The Time of the King', in *Given Time: I: Counterfeit Money*. Chicago, IL: University of Chicago Press.

Dewey, J. (1938), *Logic: The Theory of Inquiry*. New York: Holt, Rinehart, Winston.

— (1934), *A Common Faith*. New Haven, CT: Yale University Press.

— (1925), *Experience and Nature*. La Salle, IL: Open Court.

— (1916), *Democracy and Education*. Toronto: Collier-MacMillan.

Douthwaite, R. (1999), *The Growth Illusion*. Totnes, Devon, UK: Green Books.

Eliot, T. S. (1924), *The Music of Poetry*. Glasgow: Jackson, Son, and Co.

— (1943), *Four Quartets*. New York: Harcourt, Brace. Also available online at http://www.tristan.icom43.net/quartets/.

Evernden, N. (1992), *The Social Creation of Nature*. Baltimore: Johns Hopkins University Press.

Flight Pledge Union (n.d.). Retrieved 12 November 2006 from http://www.flightpledge.org.uk.

Fromm, E. (1978), *To Have or to Be?*. London: Jonathan Cape.

Golding, W. (1954), *Lord of the Flies*. London: Faber and Faber.

Goodenough, J. (2005), 'Introduction', in Read, R. and Goodenough, J. (eds), *Film as Philosophy*. London: Palgrave, 2005.

Grundy, M. (1995), 'In the Presence of God'. *Friends Journal* 41(1): 11–14.

Guetti J. (1993), *Wittgenstein and the Grammar of Literary Experience*. Athens, GA: University of Georgia Press.

Hamilton, C. (2006), *Affluenza*. London: Allen and Unwin.

— (2004), *Growth Fetish*. London: Pluto.

Harlow, E. (1992), 'The Human Face of Nature: Environmental Values and the Limits of Nonanthropocentrism'. *Environmental Ethics* 14(1): 27–42.

Heidegger, M. (1962), *Being and Time*, Macquarrie, J. and Robinson, E. (trans), New York: HarperCollins.

Hillman, M. (2004), *How We Can Save the Planet*. London: Penguin.

Jackson, P., producer/director (2003), *The Return of the King*, motion picture. USA: New Line Cinema.

— producer/director (2001), *The Fellowship of the Ring*, motion picture. USA: New Line Cinema.

Jolly, R. (1995), 'South Africa's Truth and Reconciliation Commission: Modernity and Their Discontents'. *American Philosophical Association*, 98(2): 109–15.

Judt, T., 'Bush's Useful Idiots: Tony Judt on the Strange Death of Liberal America'. *London Review of Books*, 21 September, 28(18): 3, 5.

Kovel, J. (2002), *The Enemy of Nature: The End of Capitalism or the End of the World?*. London: Zed Books.

Krog, A. (1998), *The Country of My Skull*. London: Jonathan Cape.

Kuhn, T. (1962), *The Structure of Scientific Revolutions*. Chicago, IL: University of Chicago Press.

Kundera, M. (1989), *The Art of the Novel*. New York: HarperCollins.

Long, R. (2000), *Richard Long: Artist*. [Homepage] Bristol. Retrieved 12 November 2006 from http://www.richardlong.org/.

Mamdani, M. (12 March 1998), TRC, Public Discussion, quoted in Jolly (1995), p. 113.

— (2001), 'Reconciliation without Justice', in de Vries, H. and Webe, S. (eds), *Religion and Media*. Stanford, CA: Stanford University Press, 376–87.

Manes, C. (1988), 'Philosophy and the Environmental Task'. *Environmental Ethics* 10(1): pp. 75–82.

McMaster, R. J. (1970), *Fire and Ice: an Anthology of Poetry for Mature students of the Intermediate Grades*. Don Mills, Ont., Canada: Longman.

Meadows, D. and Randers, J. and Meadows, D. (2005), *Limits to Growth*. London: EarthScan.

McGaa, E. (1990), *Mother Earth Spirituality: Native American Paths to Healing Ourselves and Our World*. New York: HarperCollins.

Monk, R. (1990), *Ludwig Wittgenstein: The Duty of Genius*. New York: Free Press.

Murphy, P. (1988), 'Sex-typing the Planet: Gaia Imagery and the Problem of Subverting Patriarchy'. *Environmental Ethics*, (10)2: pp. 155–68.

Nehamas, A. (1998), *The Art of Living*. Berkeley, CA: University of California Press.

Nix, G. (2004), *Abhorsen*. New York: HarperCollins.

— (2002), *Lirael*. New York: HarperCollins.

— (1997), *Sabriel*. New York: HarperCollins.

Orwell, G. (1961), 'Politics and the English Language', in *Collected Essays*. New York: Harcourt, Brace, pp. 355–66. Also available online at http://www.mtholyoke.edu/acad/intrel/ orwell46.htm (retrieved 12 November 2006).

— (1952), *Homage to Catalonia*. New York: Harcourt, Brace.

Pahl, G. (1995), 'Christocentric and Universalist Friends: Moving beyond the Stereotypes'. *Friends Journal* 41(1): 11–14.

Plato (n.d.) *Euthyphro* on *Internet Classics*. Jowett, B. (trans). Retrieved 12 November from http://etext.library.adelaide.edu.au/mirror/classics.mit.edu/Plato/euthyfro.html.

Plumwood, V. (1988), 'Women, Humanity and Nature'. *Radical Philosophy* 48: 6–24.

Poole, S. (2006), *Unspeak*. London: Little, Brown.

Pullman, P. (2000), *The Amber Spyglass*. New York: Del Rey.

— (1997), *The Subtle Knife*. New York: Knopf.

— (1995), *The Golden Compass*. New York: Knopf.

Rawls, J. (1999), *Collected Papers*, Freeman, S. (ed). Cambridge, MA: Harvard University Press.

— (1993), *Political Liberalism*. New York: Columbia University Press.

— (1971), *A Theory of Justice*. Cambridge, MA: Harvard University Press.

Read, R. (2006), 'Is Forgiveness Ever Possible at All?', Rudrum, D. (ed), *Literature and Philosophy: A Guide to Contemporary Debates*. London: Palgrave.

— (2005), 'Barsham and Bronson (eds) *The Lord of the Rings* and Philosophy'. *Philosophical Psychology*. 18(3): 413–15.

— (2004), 'Martin Warner, *A Philosophical Study of T. S. Eliot's* Four Quartets', *Philosophical Books* 45(1): 86–9.

— (2004), 'Wittgenstein and Faulkner's Benjy: Reflections on and of Derangement', in Gibson, J. and Huemer, W. (eds), *The Literary Wittgenstein*. London: Routledge.

— (2003), 'Literature as Philosophy of Psychopathology: William Faulkner as Wittgensteinian'. *Philosophy, Psychiatry and Psychology*. 10(2): 115–24.

— (2002), 'Incommensurability 2: World Changes', in Read, R. and Sharrock, W. (eds), *Kuhn*. Cambridge: Polity.

— (2002), 'Nature, Culture, *Ecosystem*: Or the Priority of Environmental Ethics to Epistemology and Metaphysics', in Scheman, N. and O'Connor, P. (eds), *Feminist Interpretations of Ludwig Wittgenstein*. New York: Pennsylvania State Press, pp. 408–31.

— (2001), 'On Interpreting Schizophrenia via Wittgenstein'. *Philosophical Psychology* 14(4): 449–75.

— (2001), 'On Wanting to Say: "All We Need is a Paradigm"', *The Harvard Review of Philosophy* 11: 88–105.

— (2000), 'Erotic Love Considered as Philosophy of Science', *Review Journal of Philosophy and Social Science* 25(1) and (2): 35–57.

— (2000), 'Wittgenstein', *The Philosopher's Magazine* 15: 53–4.

— (2000/1), 'How I Learned to Love (and Hate) Noam Chomsky'. *Philosophical Writings* (15) and (16): 23–48.

— (1999), 'Princess Di: the Last Perfect Republican', in Baggini, J. and Stangroom, J. (eds), *The Philosophers' Snack Pack*. London: TPM, pp. 9–13.

— (1999), 'There is No Good Reason to Believe that Philosophical Counselling Will be Effective in Curing Schizophrenia'. *Contemporary Philosophy*. 20(5) and (6): 59–63.

— (1996), 'Is Forgiveness Possible? The Cases of Thoreau and Rushdie (on) (Writing) the Unforgivable'. *Reason Papers* (21): 15–35.

— (1996), 'On the Nature and Centrality of the Concept of "Practice" Among Quakers', *Quaker Religious Thought* 86 (27:4): 33–9.

— (1995), 'The *Real* Philosophical Discovery'. *Philosophical Investigations* (18)4: 362–70.

— (n.d. a) 'Contractarian Liberalism Cannot Take Future Generations Seriously: A New Argument for Egalitarianism'. Retrieved 12 November 2006 from http://rupertread. fastmail. co.uk/Future%20generations.doc.

— (n.d. b) 'The Fantasy of Safety Through Power: The Psycho-Political Philosophy of *The Lord of the Rings*'. Retrieved 12 November 2006 from http://www.uea.ac.uk/~j339/LOTR2. htm.

Read, R. and Goodenough, J. (eds) (1995), *Film as Philosophy*. London: Palgrave.

Read, R. and Hutchinson, P. (forthcoming), *The Green Manifesto*.

Read, R. and Sharrock, W. (2002), *Kuhn*. Cambridge: Polity.

Revkin, A., 'Saving the World, and Ourselves'. *Sunday Telegraph, The New York Times Supplement*, 5 November 2006: 1, 7.

Rosenbaum, R. (1998), *Explaining Hitler*. London: Macmillan.

'Society for Applied Philosophy' (n.d.), *About the Society* [Homepage] Retrieved 15 November from http://www.appliedphil.org/.

Stevens, W. (1919), 'From Pecksniffiana: Anecdote of the Jar'. *Poetry* 15:1.

— (1954), 'Thirteen Ways of Looking at a Blackbird', *Collected Poems*. New York: Knopf.

Taylor, P. (1986), *Respect for Nature: A Theory of Environmental Ethics*. Princeton, NJ: Princeton University Press.

Tickle, O., 'Wave, Wind, Sun and Tide is a Powerful Mix'. *Guardian* (12 May 2005). Retrieved 15 November 2006 from http://www.guardian.co.uk/print/0,3858,5191269-11396,00.html.

Tolkien, J. R. R. (1937), *The Hobbit: Or There and Back Again*. London: George Allen and Unwin.

— (1954), *The Fellowship of the Ring: Being the First Part of The Lord of the Rings*. London: George Allen and Unwin.

— (1954), *The Two Towers: Being the Second Part of The Lord of the Rings*. London: George Allen and Unwin.

— (1955), *The Return of the King: Being the Third Part of The Lord of the Rings*. London: George Allen and Unwin.

Tolle, E. (2005), *A New Earth*. London: Penguin.

West, C. (1989), *The American Evasion of Philosophy: A Genealogy of Pragmatism*. Madison, WI: University of Wisconsin Press.

Wittgenstein, L. (2001), *Philosophical Investigations*, 3rd edition, Anscombe, G. E. M. (ed). London: Blackwell.

— (1993), 'Lecture on Ethics', Klagge, J. and Nordmann, A. (eds), *Philosophical Occasions*. Indianapolis, IN: Hackett, pp. 37–44.

— (1978), *Culture and Value*, von Wright, G. H. (ed), Winch, P. (trans), Chicago, IL: University of Chicago Press.

— (1972), *Lectures and Conversations on Aesthetics, Psychology and Religious Belief*, Barrett, C. (ed). Berkeley, CA: University of California Press.

— (1969), *On Certainty*. Oxford: Blackwell.

— (1922), *Tractatus Logico-Philosophicus*, Pears, D. F. and McGuiness, B. F. (trans), London: Kegan Paul.

Woodin, M. and Lucas, C. (2004), *Green Alternatives to Globalization: A Manifesto*. London: Pluto.

Young, T. (1995), ' "A project to be realized": Global Liberalism and Contemporary Africa', *Millennium: Journal of International Studies* 24(3): 527–46.

Index